IRON JOE BOB

Also by Joe Bob Briggs:

Joe Bob Goes to the Drive-In

A Guide to Western Civilization, or My Story

Joe Bob Goes Back to the Drive-In

The Cosmic Wisdom of Joe Bob Briggs

By John Bloom:

Evidence of Love (with Jim Atkinson)

IRON JOE BOB

By Joe Bob Briggs

THE ATLANTIC MONTHLY PRESS
NEW YORK

Published simultaneously in Canada
Printed in the United States of America

Library of Congress Cataloging-in-Publication Data

Briggs, Joe Bob.
    Iron Joe Bob / by Joe Bob Briggs.
    ISBN 0-87113-488-8
    1. Briggs, Joe Bob.   2. American wit and humor.   I. Title.
  PN6162.B72   1992   818'.5407—dc20   92-30426

Design by Laura Hough

The Atlantic Monthly Press
19 Union Square West
New York, NY 10003

First printing

To Bobby Bly

Contents

CONTENTS

Introduction

ll right, guys, listen up.

It hasn't been our century, has it?

We kinda blew it, didn't we?

Even though you don't know exactly what I'm talking about, you kinda *know what I'm talking about,* don't you?

Haven't you had that morning where you wake up, look around, and go, "Do I have to do this again?" And maybe you can't describe exactly what it is that's missing, but *something* is missing, right?

I'm here to tell you what's missing.

Your Ancient Spear is missing.

Missing is not quite the word. Maybe your Spear is broken, or maybe it's sagging in the middle, or maybe it's gotten soft, or maybe you just forgot how to use it. It doesn't matter. We'll get into the mythological aspects later, and you'll learn to Resurrect the Broken Spear, Mend the Sagging Ur-Spear, Launch the Warrior Spear, and, of course, Spear the Psychic Fish. But right now it's enough to know that—well, let's put it this way: you're out of touch with your Spear.

INTRODUCTION

Now what do I mean by that? Obviously I don't mean that you need to go out and buy a spear. If it was that easy, I'd be selling you a spear. Instead, I'm selling you a book.

No, what I'm talking about is something deeper, much deeper than a plain wooden spear, or even a fancy iron spear with a poison arrow on the end, or one of those spears with a lot of feathers hanging off it like Cochise had. Yes, what I'm talking about is richer than that, *richer even than Michael Ansara's spear.* I'm talking about the Golden Spear that lies at the bottom of the Soggy Gooey Lake.

Your true Spear is stuck in the mythic muck. All you have to do to get it back is read this book, understand this book, then start scooping the muck out of your psychic mind-swamp one bucket at a time. I'll never forget an experience I had one summer at a men's consciousness-raising sweat farm in western Nebraska. One Wednesday afternoon, after the ritual foot-odor smelling, a thirty-eight-year-old man from somewhere in the Midwest came up to me and he said, "Today I hated my father fully, and I remembered something he said to me once. He said, 'In or out! In or out! We can't air-condition the whole world!' And I realized for the first time how true that is. We *can't* air-condition the whole world, even though we try to do that every day of our adult male lives." We wept together for a moment, and I said to him, "You now know what it means to scoop the muck of rodents." By the end of the summer, that man had touched his Spear for the first time.

My point is that men don't know these things anymore. Men have lost touch with their Spears, their Maces, their Battering Rams, and what have they replaced them with? Weed-Eaters.

We men fought an entire war in Europe so that a New Man could emerge in America, and what did we end up with?

Ward Cleaver. Weed-Eater Man.

Let's face it, it's been all downhill since then, hasn't it?

INTRODUCTION

We're weenies.

We've *been* weenies.

Women have known this for a long time.

It took us longer to figure it out. It normally takes us at least twenty years in a relationship just to admit that when we were kids we liked to get the empty toilet paper roll and play it like a trumpet. So when you get to anything more serious than that, it takes a major life-changing cataclysmic experience, like six weeks in alcohol rehab, before we'll even *begin* to say anything like "I am a weenie. I have never had a firm conviction, or even an opinion I cared about, in my entire life."

So lemme say it right here and get it over with:

WEENIES!

That's us.

We can face up to it now.

We've got to. The future of the human race depends on it. After all, half of us turned gay in the seventies. (By the way, women are always walking around saying, "What! He's gay!" Or "How can they all be gay?" Or "Boy, would I like to grapple with *his* hematoma—but he's *gay*, can you believe that, all the *good ones* are *gay!*" Aren't you a little sick of this? The next time you hear women talking like this, please tell em, "How do you think he got to be gay *in the first place!* He tried all the other combinations and they were *boring!*")

Anyhow, that's not the point. I didn't mean to get off on that. We'll talk about that later, in the chapter on tribal rituals in Ecuador, especially the one where the rural Matsuhara jungle-dwellers lead all the young men into the woods, beat them across the hiney for three days with bulrushes until red welts appear, ram iron spikes through their elbows, stuff peyote in their mouth until they comprehend "the night wailing of the jaguar," and get em so drunk that they dance around nekkid in a sexual frenzy. What's interesting about it is that not a single Matsuhara

3

has ever become a homosexual, even though the formal pink muumuu is their principal form of male tribal dress. What does happen, however, is that all the American anthropologists living with the Matsuhara *do* become homosexual, and, in fact, many of them have been taken as wives by young Matsuhara tribal chieftains.

So anyhow, my point was that half the American men went gay in the seventies. *Then* half the American women went gay in the eighties. Pretty soon, I'm sure you can understand how, especially if they taught fractions at your junior high, eventually those numbers can result in a) a decline in population, and b) a rise in panty-hose sales. Both things are good for the economy, unless you own a topless bar in Pittsburgh. But certain things we know and love about this country, like male underwear that has funny faces on it, might quickly become a thing of the past.

All right, that's enough on lesson number one, which is, "You're a weenie."

Until you accept that, this book will be of no use to you whatsoever. It's just like AA. You've got to say that and *mean it* or we can't go on.

Here, I'll wait.

I realize I'm dealing with a lot of thirty-four-year-old fat guys still living at home, watching too much *Star Trek* and leaving Doritos crumbs on their pillows. So I'll wait a little longer.

All right, have we all said it? Good.

Lesson number two: YOU DON'T HAVE TO BE A WEENIE!

I mean it. It's not too late.

Just because your dad spent his whole life building a toolshed, buying tools, putting the tools in the toolshed, repairing the toolshed, enlarging the toolshed—you know what I'm talking about, don't you? this thing that dads do where they keep buying tools but they never *do anything* with the tools?—just because your dad did this doesn't mean *you* have to do it.

Think about it. How many times have you watched thirty-seven college basketball games in a row on ESPN and then thought to yourself, "Who was that? Was it Villanova or Vanderbilt? Georgetown or George Washington?" You're disoriented. You're confused. You're starting to feel out of control. So what do you do? *Go to a basketball game!*

How many times have you gone to the Ace Hardware store and bought $340 worth of stuff for the yard, including mulch, a tiller, a wheelbarrow-load of sod, and one of those automatic poison-spraying devices that hooks onto your garden nozzle—and then realized, when you got home, that you still had all the same stuff from *last year* stacked up in your garage? You're reeling. You're wasted. You're losing the battle with modern civilization.

How many times have you read about bizarre sexual practices and said to yourself, "I wonder if people really do that, or if they just make that stuff up to confuse people like me?"

All of these common ailments are part of being a weenie, but expressed in each one is the desire to *stop* being a weenie. But it's not enough just to finish the toolshed. It's not enough to start *using* the tools. It's not enough to remember the Vanderbilt score or spray poison on the Saint Augustine.

And, in fact, if you're reading all this and still thinking, "Wait a minute, I'll ask my wife," then you're *not* getting it yet.

You can't just *decide* to stop being a weenie. The weenie lobe of the brain is buried deep in the cerebellum, where other people can't see it. And there's only one way to get rid of it.

Surgery.

Massive life-threatening surgery.

INTRODUCTION

You've got to cut it out.

That's how I want you to think of this book. We're gonna be cutting out that weenie lobe and replacing it with a new Mature Male nervous system. This book is a shortened home-study version of my famous series of Wild Man Manliness Seminars, which have been attended by thousands of weenies already. In fact, the first time I went on a Wild Man Weekend, it changed my own life forever. You know what I'm talking about? One of those things where you go out in the woods with twenty other guys and put bandanas on your head and beat tom-toms together to prove you're not a wimp?

I'll never forget it. I sweated a lot. I cried. I sweated *while* I was crying. Of course, I was crying because they made me sweat so much. We had this one part of the weekend where we went in a giant sauna and turned it up to about, oh, 280, until everybody's skin turned the color of strawberry Jell-O and the veins in our foreheads started exploding, and it turned into this communal out-of-body *male* thing, where everybody was screaming "I want *out* of my body!" Unfortunately Saul Steinman didn't make it through that part of the weekend. Saul was a fine insurance adjuster from Milwaukee who got a brain hemorrhage and died. We'll miss him. But what was great about that is that we got to have the ancient dead-warrior ritual, where we piled stones on top of Saul's body and set him on fire, and then we started *really* feeling like men.

Are you starting to sense what I'm talking about here? Put that Dorito down and listen. It's the Masculine Movement, where we get back in touch with our caveman selves. It's so *powerful.* You really can't understand it unless you've been there, but when I got finished with my first Wild Man Weekend, I didn't wanna bathe for at least two years. And normally I would wanna bathe once every two weeks. It changes you that much.

The Wild Man process involves five basic phases: Sweating,

INTRODUCTION

Yelling, Crying, Drum Beating, and Ripping Your Shirt Off Even If It's Expensive.

You may wonder why we do this stuff. It's because the modern American male has lost touch with his primitive self. They used to have a ceremony called Separating from the Mother. (Of course, they still do. It's called the "Get a job!" ceremony.) But now most guys *never* separate from their mothers. They think *all* women are their mothers, and so they expect all their girlfriends to take care of their emotional needs.

Once I understood this, I called up my mother to tell her I was separating from her.

"That's nice," she said. "I'm glad you have a hobby."

The other ceremony they used to have is called Initiation into the Company of Men. Of course, we still have this one, too. It's called "beer." In primitive times they would ram crooked sticks through your breast, like in *A Man Called Horse,* and then beat you with a Lincoln Log or something until you felt like a man. But the modern American man never does this, and so he spends his whole life feeling *uncomfortable* around other men and never talking to them about anything except football.

I hope you're following this.

That's why we start off with the lobster-sauna Sweating Ceremony. Then we move on to the Yelling Like Banshees Ceremony. Then we sit in a circle, and whoever has the stick gets to talk, and he's supposed to say stuff from *A Chorus Line,* like "I was always afraid I was a homosexual, and my father kicked my Tonka dumptruck when I was seven and I never got over it," until he starts bawling like a baby in front of everybody else.

Next comes Beating the Manly Tom-Tom. In order to get in touch with our real Wild Man self, we whale away on these drums and slamdance against trees until we lose control and *become the drum.* It took me a while to understand that part. At my first Wild Man Weekend, I lost control and started giving noogies to Fred

Bushman, a Xerox marketing analyst from Tampa, Florida. Sometimes guys get so carried away they start screaming out personal stuff, from the deepest part of the primitive brain lobe, like "She divorced me because I never could stand her sister!"

And finally we get to the Ceremony of the Ripping Shirt, where we cavort around like apes in the jungle, revealing our manliness to other men, becoming the true warrior-king-lover-gods that we always were but Brenda Weatherby in tenth grade would never believe it. Then we make a conga line and dance out into the woods and plunge into the river and splash around like alligator gar on cocaine until we feel manly enough to take off all our clothes and rip the guts out of a wild hog.

I felt so much better after doing this the first time. I went back to Grapevine, Texas, where I live, and I told my girlfriend Wanda Bodine everything I'd been through, and she said, "That sounds great. Did they teach you how to wear the same color sock on both feet?"

You ever feel like women don't *understand* just how manly we are?

It bugs me.

Anyhow, that's not the point. The point is that *you* could have all these same Wild Man experiences that I had. And I know what you're thinking, right at this very moment. You're thinking, "I ain't getting nekkid in the woods."

Don't worry about it. Really. That'll come later. Some men never go beyond flesh-toned jockstraps, but we don't hold it against em.

All I want you to know right now is that, if you'll trust me, if you'll clear your head, get rid of your old weenie preconceptions, give me a little slack, then by the time you finish this book you'll feel a new male *power* rising inside you. You'll feel manly as you've never felt manly before. You'll feel the whole course of manly civilization rushing through your manly veins.

INTRODUCTION

You'll know what it's like to Straighten the Broken Spear. You'll never feel like a wimp or a loser or a weakling again, for the rest of your life. We're gonna do this together. We're gonna be men. And *how* are we gonna do it? By doing the most manly thing that men can do together:

I'll tell you a fairy tale.

It'll be fun, really.

It's a good one.

It has a beautiful princess in it.

You're not buying this, are you?

Turn the goldurn page.

The Legend of the Limp Spear

The Krankaway Indians of Far West Texas told a legend about a warrior called He of the Full Loins. They would recite this legend once a year at the Ceremony of the Sagging Buttock, where the village elders would gather naked around the fire and wail for their dead mothers. Kit Carson, the famous western scout, witnessed this ritual at a Krankaway village near present-day Hudspeth County, and he described it as follows:

"All the boys in the tribe were gagged and trussed like captive livestock and placed in circles around the ceremonial space. The chief went to each young man with a hot poker, threatening to burn out their tongues if they so much as uttered a single peep. Sometimes, after the chief had passed a certain boy, the boy would say 'Peep.' After that boy was pummeled about the head and shoulders, the ceremony would begin. The eldest warrior chanted the story, accompanied by a lone drummer, and the telling would sometimes go on all night long. This was mainly because the eldest warrior would sometimes be in his nineties, and so he'd have to excuse himself every five minutes. Let's not dwell on it."

The first part of the tale went as follows:

> *A young boy lived far to the south, beyond the land of the Toltec, the Mixtec, and the Aztec. One day, while walking in the valley belonging to a great princess, he discovered a piece of rope on the path. He bent over to pick it up, but at the moment he touched it he felt a sharp pain in his right side. He dropped the rope quickly and left it lying in a heap, curled up in the dirt, for horses to stomp on.*

Sound familiar?

How often have you felt your own limp rope lying in a heap, being stomped on by wild stallions?

Clearly there's a lot more going on here than just a story about a boy and his limpness, though. Why does he come from the south? Why does the valley belong to a princess? And why the pain in his right side and not his left? All myths tell us something about ourselves, and this one is especially rich in what it has to say about our modern limp rope and the sharp pain it causes us when we attempt to pick it up.

So let's take a look at that rope—where it's been, what's happened to it, what disgusting places it's been hanging out in. And to do that, we need to look first at the complete history of Manhood, in one easy-to-read time chart:

> **500,000 B.C.:** In order to prove his manhood, a man must wrestle a twelve-ton hairy mammoth to the ground with his bare hands, bash its head in with a rock, rip the flesh from its bones, eat until he's full, give the rest of the meat to his tribe, and carve a picture of the mammoth on his chest with a dull flint.

250,000 B.C.: To prove his manhood, a man must sleep on a bed of hot coals for three days when he's fourteen years old, then attack an enemy tribe armed with nothing but a handmade spear. If he lances thirty men, pillages all their goods, and makes off with their women, he is a man.

100,000 B.C.: To prove he's a man, he must trek 200 miles into a dense wilderness, fending off wild beasts, until he arrives at a sanctuary to the god Urgel. After fasting for twenty-four days and sacrificing ninety rams and thirty bullocks, he asks the god Urgel to protect him and make him a man, then returns 350 miles on icy rivers in a birch-bark canoe.

5,000 B.C.: A real man must know how to kill with his bare hands, command an army, possess any woman he desires, discipline a herd of wild steeds, crack the whip over a slave galley, and rout the Mongols from the grassy steppe.

500 B.C.: A man must possess a household of loyal wives and servants who trust his wisdom, his learning, and his ability to gain favor at court. He receives tribute from fiefdoms in distant countries, and he studies geometry and philosophy at the school of Plato. He is a great public speaker and commands the attention of all who hear him.

100 A.D.: To prove he's a man, he must have a knowledge of the sports arena. He owns gladiators and chariots, and he spends great sums on a house full of pillars and altars. He knows all the religions, and he believes most of them.

1000 A.D.: To prove his manhood, he must journey great distances with armies and destroy other nations so that his nation might be the strongest in the world. He can spend months in a small boat on the ocean, or years managing campaigns against the Hun or the Vandal. He insists on his "honor," and will protect it with a sword.

1300 A.D.: To be a man, he must drive the Arab hordes out of the Holy Land. He accumulates armies and cities and wealth by burning, looting, and killing, and when he is challenged, he slices men's heads off with a broadsword. But he also knows music and poetry, which he uses to woo women.

1700 A.D.: To prove his manhood, a man must own property and father children and gain favor from the king. His family name must be established as worthy and honorable, and he must carry on the traditions established by his forefathers.

1800 A.D.: To prove his manhood, a man must own property and father children and hate the king. He must serve in the army and the government, and he must prove himself worthy by serving his country.

1900 A.D.: To be a man, he must own his own business and father children and provide for them and for his wife, so that they never lack anything. He must serve his country in time of war.

1910 A.D.: To be a man, he must have his own business, father children, provide for his family, and pay taxes.

1920 A.D.: To be a man, he must father children, provide for his family, pay taxes, and own a car.

1930 A.D.: To be a man, he must father children, work at a job at least sixty hours a week, provide for his family, and vote.

1940 A.D.: To be a man, he must have a family and have a job.

1950 A.D.: To be a man, he must have a family, have a job, have a car, and own a TV set.

1960 A.D.: To be a man, he must own a TV set, root

for a sports team, own a car he can't afford, and have a job that he occasionally complains about to his wife.

1965 A.D.: To be a man, he must own a TV set, a stereo, season tickets to his local sports teams, two cars, a job that he hates but that pays really well, and a wife that can shut up if she doesn't like it.

1970 A.D.: To prove his manhood, he has to be able to tell his boss he's quitting.

1975 A.D.: To prove his manhood, he has to be able to tell his wife he wants a divorce.

1980 A.D.: To prove his manhood, he has to have at least one girlfriend who doesn't expect anything from him, the right to watch sports on TV all weekend if he wants to, and a car that costs more than his yearly income. In his job he's not a man unless he can ask for a raise without feeling guilty.

1985 A.D.: To prove his manhood, a man must be able to contradict his girlfriend about what restaurant they're going to eat at.

1990 A.D.: To prove his manhood, he must be able to ask his boss for permission to go to the restroom.

1992 A.D.: To prove his manhood, he must be able to ask his girlfriend for a twenty-dollar-a-week allowance.

So there you have it. Manhood through the ages. An awesome human spectacle.

But back to our story. Fortunately the young brave, unlike the American male of 1992, didn't leave the limp rope lying beside the road. Let's see what he can teach us, as the legend continues:

When the young boy saw that the limp rope was being withered and frayed by the constant trod of livestock, he dared to pick it up a second time. But he grabbed

14

it too quickly, and it cut a deep burn on the fat part of his hand.

Have you ever felt like you were being punished for merely *touching* your limp rope?

And yet, if we don't touch it, it will be destroyed by pigs on their way to market.

I don't think we need to go far to find the emotional meaning here. I can't tell you how many men I meet who have *abandoned their rope* on the dusty roadway. They've never even *tried* to pick it up a second time. And I can't tell you how many *more* men have burned their hands and felt guilty about it.

Do you ever wonder what's going on when the smiling gentleman who sells you avocados at the corner grocery is suddenly discovered one night dressed up like Morgan Fairchild, screaming, "Take me now, Geraldo Rivera!"

This is simply a man who has been burned by the limp rope and doesn't know what else to do.

Here's another way to think about it. I keep getting these letters in the mail about when Jesus is coming to town. I realize that a person who's on nine thousand mailing lists is gonna get hassled by a lot of people whose elevators don't go all the way to the top floor, but it's the *number* of these warnings that's getting to me.

This one guy in Glendale, California, keeps writing to me about how the Virgin Mary recently had a gig in Flushing Meadows, New York, where she criticized tabloid journalism and predicted a Los Angeles earthquake. I wrote back to him, pointing out that I have also criticized tabloid journalism and predicted a Los Angeles earthquake, so could there be some possibility that the Virgin Mary is communicating with me without my knowledge? But he never has written me back.

There's another group of "Jesus Is Coming" true believers

who have been hanging out in Yugoslavia, because the Virgin Mary appeared there several times and told them to love one another. (I wrote to them to ask whether they would still be hanging out there if the Virgin Mary had appeared and told them to *hate* one another? I mean, you're either gonna *follow instructions* or you're not. No answer from there, either.)

For a while there was a guy on an independent TV station out of Irving, Texas, who was explaining *exactly* where each prophecy in the Book of Revelations would be fulfilled in the next ten years, with references to a Middle East war, nuclear holocaust, and the comeback of the miniskirt. This guy vanished for lack of funding.

I'm not even gonna mention the Adventists. They've been predicting the date Jesus would show up for almost a hundred years now, but the last time he didn't show they changed the date to "soon." I think this shows a remarkable theological shift from the specific to the general, and probably guarantees an increase in membership for at least the next decade.

In other words, a whole lotta people are waiting on Him. And, because of that, a few might wanna know what you can do to get ready. Because this is the game we always used to play back at the Babtist church in Grapevine, Texas, where I grew up: "What do I want Jesus to see me doing when he comes back?"

Most of the religious brochures make very vague suggestions about how to get ready. "Repent" is the most popular one. "Clean your household" is one mentioned by a Pennsylvania evangelist. This is one that my mother would like. But most of us are too screwed up to even know what those things mean. I mean, we're all dressed up like Morgan Fairchild, screaming "Geraldo, take me now!" Maybe we're not *literally* dressed up like Morgan Fairchild, but that's what we're doing. So I have very *specific* suggestions for the coming Event. You might wanna keep these tacked up on your refrigerator.

1. When Jesus comes, it would not be a good idea to be wearing black leather and latex and holding a riding crop in your hand.

2. When the Messiah shows up and you're in a synagogue, continue the same prayers, but add the following words at the end of every verse: "Correct me if I'm wrong."

3. When the Messiah shows up, and you're in a Babtist church, it's probably not a good idea to say "Would you like me to point out the ones that are going to hell?"

4. When the Messiah shows up, and you're in a Methodist church, refrain from saying "Whatever you tell us, we'll put it to a vote and probably go with your program."

5. When the Messiah shows up, and you've been machine-gunning Kurdish peasants, it's not a good idea to say "But that was a long time ago."

6. When the Messiah shows up in a Unitarian church, try not to say "We're all equals here. Don't expect any special privileges."

7. When the Messiah shows up and you're watching ESPN, don't ask him to wait until halftime.

8. When the Messiah shows up and you're pursuing an acting career, don't tell him you want to explore how your character will respond to this.

9. When the Messiah shows up at Willem Dafoe's house, don't say "I *knew* I was off on the accent."

10. When the Messiah shows up at the one time in your life when you're doing something decent, like feeding the poor, don't say "Can you wait just a minute? I need to finish up this act of human kindness here and then I'll be right with you."

You get the idea?

If any of us started playing the What Do We Do If Jesus Comes game today, *we'd be screwed!* Because we're all Zombie People. The whole generation.

You ever get out your high school yearbook and find pictures of zombies in there?

Or maybe you'd call em ghost people. They're people you remember. You know *exactly* who they are. Some of em you spent twelve years of your life with. You saw em almost every day. But when you see the face now, you feel *nothing.* Zip. You hear no voice. You have no memories of anything you said to them or they said to you. You could get more excited when you see the face on a Betty Crocker package. And if you hadn't picked up the yearbook, you would never *ever* have remembered that this person was alive.

It's like they exist but they don't exist. They drift into the room, drift out of the room, never make an impression, hang around, have a couple beers, and now they're out there somewhere, bearing children or something—only their gynecologist doesn't notice them either. In the thirties people called em "wallflowers." But that's way too flashy a description for these people. "Linoleum people" is what they are.

But here's the scary part. It's not "them" at all. *You* are the Linoleum Person. *I* am a zombie, too. We're *all* people with massive American Express bills and nowhere to go.

Everybody between the ages of thirty and fifty should get out their high school yearbooks. Thirty to fifty is prime time, right? These are the people that should be running the country, building stuff, handing out jobs, right? These are the people that are supposed to kick hiney against the Japanese whiz kids and the German Doitchie Boys. Right?

Look in those yearbooks: Zombie People.

Thirty-eight-year-old guys that got divorced and moved back

home to live with Mom. Guys that did so many drugs between 1967 and 1979 that they have little lines around their eye sockets, from buggin em out so often. "Performance artists" who have never made more than twenty bucks a night for their entire fifteen-year careers. Fat guys who watch too much *Star Trek*. All the people on *Love Connection*. Guys that sell insurance for ten years, then freak out when they realize they're getting old and they *haven't ever been to New Zealand*.

You know the kind of mindset I'm talking about here?

They looked like zombies in 1970, they remained zombies in 1980, and they're gonna be zombies in the *next* century, too. On the outside, they may be cruising down Santa Monica Boulevard in a Jag. On the inside, they're thinking, "Maybe I could grow a ponytail and get a guest shot on *21 Jump Street*. That's still on, isn't it? I gotta watch more TV. I gotta go on a diet and watch more TV."

There hasn't been a generation like this since the time when the emperor of Rome was a transvestite. (Emperor Elagabalus, for the scholars out there.)

It's not like anybody *we know* is out there designing new tool-and-die plants that the Germans have to spy on. It's not like Lisa Salvatini, from your eleventh-grade biology class, suddenly devoted herself to science and developed a new strain of hybrid wheat that will feed the Russians for the next ten years.

What the heck have we got to *sell* anybody?

But what's amazing is that we're like a pit bulldog who's had all his legs cut off, but he still *believes* he can fight. We still think we can lay around the house all day, watching TV, and then tomorrow we can put on a suit and go downtown and convince somebody, with our *charm,* to hire us.

That's why America now has only *one* product that the whole world wants: movies.

We're great bullstuff artists.

But you can only listen to the charming bullstuff for so long before you have to tell a guy, "That was great, but now *we* have to get back to work."

You know what I'm talking about?

Let's get our butts in gear.

Right now.

Turn the goldurn page.

Yanking the Sacred Rope

T he legend continues:

The young boy sat beside the road, nursing his burned hand, when suddenly a beautiful princess came riding by on a pony.

"What are you doing?" she asked him.

Gold glistened from her hair.

"Trying to pick up the rope," he said.

"But you've already done it," she told him.

The young boy looked down, and there was the rope, in his hand.

How many times have you found yourself standing around with your rope in your hand?

I think we can all relate to this.

There comes a time in every man's life when the rope just kind of takes over on him. From about the age of fourteen to the age of twenty-four, you don't swing the rope—the rope swings you. But what I want you to know is that it's *important* to let that rope go where it wants to go.

A hundred years ago I wouldn't have had to point this out. Men knew about ropes and roping. But these days I have to spell it out. That's why we have the institution called spring break, and why, every year, I diligently compile the annual *Joe Bob Briggs Guide to the Top Five Party Schools in America.* I spent a whole heck of a lot of time researchin it this year, gettin drunk with numerous brain-damaged Professors of Wood Alcohol. And the only students eligible to advise me on the selections must have

a. a criminal record

b. the ability to "gator" while sober

c. a minimum of three "incompletes" from fall semester, three failing courses as of March 1, and at least nine hours credit from the sociology department

This year's results, in reverse order, are:

The *fifth* best party school in America is . . .
University of Northern Colorado.
This is the only one in the top five I have not personally inspected, but their reputation for wild-dog bestiality, especially in the coed housing, has spread four states away and caused me to include em even if they're just amazing liars. Here's the facts:

Where is it? Greeley, Colorado.

Where's that? I don't know.

What do I have to do to get in? Score a solid 230 on your SATs.

Drink of choice? Triple-tequila lizard-tail shooters.

Spring break destination? Palm Springs, where they all hang around Bob Hope Boulevard going, "Wanna go chop down a palm tree and moon some girls in Spandex lift-and-separate body stockings?" (Country boys.)

Rating: Four kegs on a ten-keg scale.

Numero Four-o: University of Virginia

The former home of Kappa Alphas able to bite the heads off muskrats and juggle magnums at the same time, these guys have slipped a couple notches in recent years.

Where is it? Charlottesville, Virginia.

What do I have to do to get in? Have a daddy named anything "the third."

Drink of choice? Crème de Mr. Potato Head.

Spring break destination? Lauderdale, where you can recognize em as the ones with twitchy lips and the keys to Jaguars they left in Georgia someplace 'cause "I don't remember, Officer."

Rating: Six kegs.

Numero Three-o: University of Arkansas

It gets lonely in the Ozarks, so the official university drinkin age is fourteen. In January three guys took eight cases of Coors into a dorm room on the west side of the campus and didn't come out for six days. They failed to set the record.

Where is it? Fayetteville, Arkansas.

What do I have to do to get in? Repeat after me: "Whooooooooooo pig sooey." If you can say this accurately, you're in.

Drink of choice? "A big ole Bud, unless we don't have a Bud, and then a big ole Coors, unless we don't have a Coors, and then a big ole Old Milwaukee tall boy, unless we don't have . . ." Remember, we're talkin Ozarks.

Spring break destination? South Padre Island, Texas. They're the guys crammed in the Broncos, cuttin donuts on the national seashore and trying to rip the bikini off any girl named Wilma.

Rating: Eight kegs.

Numero Two-o: The State University of New York at Stony Brook

A newcomer to the list, these zoo animals have an annual student competition called Let's Get Handicapped Day. This year's winner consumed seven undiluted bags of Arkansas Polio Weed and achieved total paralysis.

Where is it? Somewhere out on Long Island.

What do I have to do to get in? Talk through your nose and tip the admissions counselor a twenty. (It's New York.)

Drink of choice? Brandy Alexander Graham Bell. (After you drink it, you spend the night punchin MCI numbers until you find one you can steal, then you call thirty-seven foreign countries.)

Spring break destination? Any motel with an average temperature above 55. (*Nasty* girls.)

Rating: Ten kegs.

And finally, this year's grand champion party school: **Northern Arizona University.**

Recently set the world record for something called "alcohol probation" when three entire dorms spray-painted the resident hall director and distributed Coors twelve-packs to every single member of a forty-eight-member sorority in return for something called "grease-monkey window dancing." I don't know what it is, but I don't condone it, and I'd like some.

Where is it? Flagstaff, Arizona, up in the mountains.

What do I have to do to get in? Find it.

Drink of choice? The Grand Canyon Cooler, made from a Mescalero Indian recipe used for pregnancy tests.

Spring break destination? Rocky Point, Mexico. I'm not kidding. They make caravans for Sombrero-Land, Boys Town, Hasta

La Vistaville, and play the old college game Don't Worry about It, *We're Americans!* Afterward they have a memorial service for the victims.

Rating: Off the scale.

Sometimes people are surprised to hear this knowledge coming from me. Not many people know that I used to be a member of a fraternity. I don't like to talk about it. But, yes, I was a Sigma Nu at Tarleton State cow college in Stephenville, Texas, for a full three weeks. Or, as we used to say in the old "frat":

"My name is Scumface Pledge Briggs, sir, and yes, sir, I would like to wear those plastic baby diapers on the outside of my clothes all day, sir."

I mean, who could resist this level of male bonding? Everybody going around *together* wearing plastic baby diapers while sucking down Old Milwaukee tall boys by the case. I'm surprised I didn't become a homosexual.

Anyhow, I'd probably still be a practicing Sigma Nu today, except for two things:

1. I got kicked out of Tarleton State when I flunked rodeo the third time.

2. I killed one of my pledge brothers on Barfhead Weekend.

When I killed my brother, who was named Slats Franken, it had a definite effect on everyone's mood. We even canceled the annual Butt Toss, which, if you've ever been a Sigma Nu, you know is a sacred and secret ceremony that I can't go into here.

But I guess enough time has passed so that I can talk about what really happened, even though it's not easy. Barfhead Weekend, as you probably know, is the annual Sigma Nu festival where we force ugly girls to get down on their hands and knees and form a mule train, then the pledges dress up like Mexican tour guides and sell rides to upperclassmen. It's a harmless little bit of fraternity whimsy.

But one of the things outsiders don't know about Barfhead Weekend is that one pledge is always singled out to be the Epileptic Reetard. It's an honor awarded to the pledge who has distinguished himself by carrying the most Jell-O Pudding under his armpits in the previous Thursday night's Cosby Run. Slats Franken was that year's winner. The poor little guy had armpits so hollow you could have hidden a stuffed mongoose in there.

So anyhow, the job of the Epileptic Reetard is to run into the room with your shirt off sometime after the official Barfhead Mule Train is formed and start twisting around on the floor like a wounded grizzly bear with rabies, while all the other guys yell "Stand back! It's Slats! He has permanent brain damage and a rare epileptic disorder! Just leave him alone! Give him air!" And then the Epileptic Reetard jumps up off the floor and starts attacking innocent bystanders, smearing a special axle-grease paste all over their legs, arms, and clothing.

Just a little practical joke. It's the kind of thing we do in fraternities because it fosters goodwill, brotherhood, togetherness, and values that will serve us well in later life. It probly made me what I am today.

But this year was different. Right before it was time to go on, Slats came to me—he already had his axle-grease mixed up, his shirt was off, and foam was starting to seep out of the corners of his mouth—he came to me and he said, "Joe Bob, I have a *premonition* about tonight."

And I said, "What do you mean, a premonition?"

And he said, "I don't think I can be the Epileptic Reetard."

"Sure you can do it. If I've ever seen a *natural* Epileptic

Reetard, it's the man who sticks pencils up his nose to amuse himself."

"Yeah, I know," Slats told me, "normally I would think that, too. But tonight I'm just afraid that if I do the Epileptic Reetard, I'll like it so much that I'll . . . well . . ."

"Yeah? What, Slats?"

"That I'll never come back."

"Come back?"

"I didn't expect you to understand. But I have one favor to ask you."

"What's that?"

"If I start to go over the edge, if I go into the seizure and I lose my ability to stop twitching, I want you to give me these pills."

He poured out some green and white pills into my hand.

"What are these?" I asked him.

"They'll calm me down."

"But what are they?"

"Just some depressants. They'll calm me down."

And that was the last time I talked to Slats.

That night the Epileptic Reetard routine started off without a hitch. Slats came in twitching like a pro, practically mashed his face in when he hit the floor, started rooting around on the sides of his arms like Curly, screamed like a Zulu warrior, and had the mule train girls so scared that three of em were clinging to light poles. But after this went on for about ten minutes, I knew something was wrong. I knew Slats had gone *over the edge.* I knew he had passed from Epileptic Reetard state to Paranoid-Schizophrenic Frontal-Lobotomy Candidate right before our eyes.

And so I rushed in to administer the Quaaludes, but before I got there I shuddered in horror and stopped to watch:

Shirley "the Weasel" Stoddard, chubbiest girl in the mule

train, took a baseball bat to Slats—hit him about eighty times before we got her to stop.

Later we asked Shirley why she did it. It turned out Shirley was permanently brain damaged and prone to epileptic fits *and* dyslexic. She thought she was caressing herself. Actually she was beating the brains out of another person.

After I got back from taking Shirley to the Terrell State Institute for the Feeble-Minded, I reflected on my life. I could have stopped Slats that night. I could have said, "Slats, don't worry about it. I'll do the Epileptic Reetard tonight." And then Shirley the Weasel would have beaten *my* brains out with a baseball bat. And Slats could have had a long productive life as a . . . now that I think about it, Slats didn't have diddly-squat worth of a life ahead of him. Good thing the little nerd died early.

And that's just *one* of the valuable life lessons I learned during my career as a frat man.

And, while we're on the subject, I've gotta say something else about the way good old-fashioned male initiation rites are being undermined in this country. I was such a devoted and serious college student that I have credits from thirty-seven different schools, so I think I know what I'm talking about when I say that this "no drinking on campus" stuff is just a *little bit* out of line.

One time, at the University of Arkansas, I was part of the Gang of Seven who drank ninety-four cases of Coors in one week without ever leaving a dorm room. Think about it. Besides the sheer stamina this took, we had to *smell* each other.

Another time, at Ole Miss, I was the runner-up in the annual Swill-and-Spill Kamikaze Mud Slide, where you skid on your butt down a cattle chute while trying to pour, carry, and drink a tequila shooter, chased with an Old Milwaukee tall boy. I didn't spill a drop. I would have won, but I temporarily lost my bearings and drank the tall boy first and chased it with the tequila.

I went to Cal State–Chico one time and showed the student

body how to mix more *healthful* drinks, like Jack-Daniel's-and-Diet-Dr.-Pepper. That'll keep that body fat down, save room for the keg later.

So two things I really know about are a) college and b) getting polluted in college, and so what I'd like to say, first, is we should all remember to drink *only* in moderation. I was talking to my friend Hunter Thompson about this last week, and he reminded me that crack cocaine causes *no permanent brain damage,* but you have to know when to say when. So I wanna be straight about that first of all. We're talking social drinking here.

Next, let's get down to the real nitty-gritty about why they have all these new federal laws telling the colleges that if they allow a lot of liquor on campus, they get all their money cut off.

Listen up, bozos: All those guys and gals in college are *voting age.* Why don't you ask *them* to vote on it?

Nobody would pass a law saying black people can't do something, and they can't even *vote* on whether or not they get to do it. Nobody would pass a law saying people *over* the age of sixty-five can't drink, even though it's probly *more* damaging to them than it is to people aged eighteen to twenty-one. But this particular group of people gets trampled on more than any other single minority group we've got.

So what's really going on here? Why would we have a gerbil-brained law like this that restricts personal freedom and treats voters like pond scum?

Because the lawmakers are *old,* and they just flat don't *like* teenagers. They don't like their hormones. They don't like their wildness. They don't like their lack of *control.* It's almost as if our *mothers* ran the Congress these days. Mothers have *always* wanted to totally eliminate alcohol from campuses. But who always stepped in and restored freedom?

Fathers.

Aren't any of these congressmen fathers? Are they all

transvestites? Didn't anybody read Hemingway or get drunk with his old man? When these people were eighteen, did they really believe that *they* were too stupid to make decisions about alcohol? I doubt it—because now they're sixty-two and they don't realize they're too stupid to make decisions about *restricting* alcohol.

Give these people their liquor back. It's their decision, not yours.

We'll come back to this later, but the point I wanted to make is that when the young man finds himself standing by the side of the road with a rope in his hand, he has *got* to do something with the rope. And the only way he can do something with the rope is to listen to what other men tell him.

The legend continues:

> *While the young boy stood by the side of the road, gawking at the rope, a handsome prince rode up and laughed at the sight. The prince reached down, tied the rope around the boy's neck, and rode off with the beautiful princess.*

We've all been there, right?

But don't get *depressed* about it. This is something that *has* to happen—because there's more to learning how to use your rope than just drinking a lot in college. You've also got to wear a commode on your head.

Let me illustrate what I mean.

One of the colleges I'm proud to say I attended is Texas A&M. I went there for almost one entire semester and majored in veterinary gynecology. But the main reason I decided to be an Aggie was so that I could join the Aggie Corps, the pride of Texas, the uniformed students that are even *more* serious about army stuff than regular army guys are.

To give you some idea, when we invaded Iraq last year,

there were guys in the Aggie Corps launching Patriot missiles out of their dorm windows. These guys wear medals on their *underwear.*

And that's why I can't just stand idly by while the corps is dragged through the mud with these accusations of how women cadets are treated like old pieces of dirty laundry, just wadded up and slam-dunked into a basketball clothes hamper.

Listen to me. Please try to understand this:

Everybody in the corps is treated like a disposable diaper. It's *not* discrimination. Up until 1964 the men had to stand out on the federal highway with a toilet bowl on their head, singing Scottish folk ballads in Gaelic. I was personally offended when a federal judge struck down this time-honored corps tradition by calling it "a peculiarly sadistic form of hazing."

It was *not* peculiar.

It was *genuinely* sadistic.

Nobody gets the point anymore. I'll never forget the proud day I was stripped nekkid and lashed to the underbelly of a wild hog, which was released into the Big Thicket National Wildlife Preserve. They found me nine hours later, curled up in the fetal position, licking the sap off a pine tree.

It's experiences like that that have made me what I am today. In a way, now that I think about it, I'm *always* curled up in the fetal position, licking the sap off a pine tree. Maybe it's not a *real* pine tree, and maybe I'm not *really* licking it, but in my *mind* that's what I'm doing.

Another thing. How do you know whether a cadet has leadership potential or not unless he can eat twelve Big Macs in a row, chase that with forty-seven Coronas, and walk a straight line with a blacksmith's anvil strapped to his skull? We have sick people in the Texas A&M administration today who want to *end* this practice and replace it with a written test.

I'd like to know what *questions* they're gonna ask.

"What would that thirty-seventh Corona taste like if you were drinking it right now?"

See, you can't replace *real* military experience with mere theory.

Do these women wanna be regular army or not? We already let em get by with refusing to wear the trick britches that Aggie Corpsmen have always worn to football games so that people think seventeen hundred Thurston P. Howell III look-alikes have all entered the stadium at the same time. We lightened up on the obstacle course regulations, so that they no longer have to grease their bodies and slide through a sewer pipe using only their butt muscles.

I mean, how many exceptions can you make before you lose military discipline entirely?

I ask you, what would have happened to me if the corps had never made me attach surgical clamps to the fleshy part of my . . . no, never mind about that part. I guess women couldn't do that, after all.

But I'll tell you one goldurn thing. I felt like a *soldier,* for all three of the days I was in the corps.

So this time when you're standing around with a grin on your face, fondling your own rope, or trying to get your rope off your neck, is a special time—but it's not the end of the story:

> *The young boy placed both hands firmly on the rope around his neck, yanked on it with all his strength—and there was a great burst of light as the rope was magically transformed into a bronze spear.*

In other words, the limp rope must some day become the rigid spear. And yet, time after time, we find modern men who are stuck in the limp-rope stage, unable to take their rope with both hands and yank on it. These are the men who are still hanging around singles bars at the age of forty-five. These are the men who put frogs in your locker at the health spa. These are the men who date girls named Tiffany.

And then there are many men, like me, who are constantly slipping back into the confused world of slinging the rope around, even though we attained our Spears long ago.

For example, I'm writing this in the spring. This is the time of year when everybody goes down to Mexicana Airlines, the only airline that passes out Chiclets so your eardrums won't explode when you take off and land, and buys a seventy-eight-dollar ticket to Cancún so they can lay around on the beach with somebody they can't stand and throw back Coco Locos till they puke all over their flamingo-pocket Meskin shirt. This makes you feel relaxed enough to forget the guy that just took you off afternoons in Urban Systems Planning and transferred your hiney to night shift in West Coast Management Operations and spoiled your chance to brush up against Heather Sullivan, the eighteen-year-old UCLA intern who came by once a day to file commercial inventory flow charts. If it hadn't been for that transfer, you might be lying on the beach with Heather Sullivan, but instead you're lying on the beach with Donna "Anything for a Quarter" Phelps, who looks like a frozen fish stick in a swimsuit.

You don't *really* wanna be in Cancún with Donna Phelps, but you're still "wrestling with the rope." There's still some part of you that hasn't yanked on it enough to make it the Bronze Spear.

The fun really starts on the *second* day of your Mexican adventure when Donna decides she wants to take the three-hour bus ride to the ancient Mayan city of Chicken Little, where some-body piled up some rocks and was *never seen again.* This is so much better than looking at Donna in a swimsuit that you throw back seven, eight tequila shooters, tip Paco the bus driver a thou-sand pesos to drive ninety through the jungle, and lose two of your molars on the way to the sacred temple. Once there, you spend a delightful afternoon at the Café de Azteca, sponging sweat out of your armpits and picking giant leeches off your ankles, until Donna comes back from the lecture about how this was the most advanced civilization in Mexico and they used to rip people's hearts out and eat em, and Donna says, "It's just so fascinating how they were *never seen again.*"

The third day of your Mexican dream vacation is usually the one where you decide to go up on the water-ski parachute kite pulled by a speedboat that dumps you on the beach and tears all the ligaments in your right leg. This takes care of your leisure activities through the fifth day.

On the sixth day, it's time to take the burro ride up the mountain to the waterfall, followed by the "Get Drunk on a Sailboat with a Brown-Skinned Body-Building Cliff Diver" Taco Lunch Cruise. Not much energy left for the rest of the day, so you go down to the harbor and lob cheap souvenir paperweights at the people lounging on the deck of the Love Boat.

Finally, your relaxing siesta is at an end. At the airport you browse one more time for the genuine orange and turquoise billowy beach dresses that Donna has her eye on, and you gladly fork over eighty bucks to the pleasant representative of the Cozumel Indian tribe who hand-sews every single price tag. As you bite into your homebound Chiclet, you know you've experienced another culture, and for the first time you realize one of the secrets of history, the true reason they were *never seen again.*

This, too, is necessary. After these seven days, most men are ready to get rid of the rope forever.

Come with me now.

Let's get rigid.

Launching the Spear

The next passage in the Krankaway legend has been variously interpreted, so we'll quote from the more colloquial translation of pure-blood Krankaway William T. Blueskull, professor of ethnic culture and women's sports at New Mexico Technical Institute, whose father was chief in the fifties:

> *The kid was royally pissed off about being a chump for the prince, so he speared everything in sight.*

This is what teen psychologists sometimes call the "difficult" years, when the young man learns how to buy paint in a spray can and burn down parts of Detroit. But I want us to view this transition period in a more *positive* way. All men are *really* trying to say at this point is, "I would like to kill a lot of stuff."

Fine. Let's let em sow their wild oats. All we have to do is discover what exactly should be killed.

There's one great American sport that not too many people

know how to do anymore, and that's the sport of clubbing to death and mutilating cute little froggies for fun. I highly recommend it.

It's frog-giggin' season now, as a matter of fact, and I got me a huntin lease this year down in Houston. It's one of the best municipal drainage ditches in the slushy runoff Pork Rind Bottoms area of Buffalo Bayou. It's frog-giggin' lease number 3478, in case you're down there and you wanna come by and squash a few reptiles with me and Rhett Beavers, my usual huntin partner. But for those of you going out for the first time this season, specially you young people, I wanna outline a few safety rules so nobody gets gigged to death by mistake.

1. Forget rivers. Forget lakes. Always hunt frogs in a ditch. It's cheaper, quicker, it's right behind your house, and here's the most important part—*the frogs never expect you.* This is the number one advantage you have over the frog. Always remember it.

2. Frogs are stupid. That's why the first thing you do when you wanna kill one is you shine a flashlight in their eyes. They'll sit there and wait for you to stick a three-pronged metal implement through their gizzards. This implement is called a Frog Fondue Fork. It's very painful for the frog.

3. Carry a baseball bat. I like the Louisville Slugger thirty-two-inch model, but some go for the twenty-eights due to the superior quickness and mobility of the lighter woods. The purpose of the baseball bat is to explode downward against the frog's skull, creating a sound that resembles potato salad being dropped on the linoleum. Don't worry if you throw up the first time. You will learn to love this sound.

4. Never watch a Walt Disney movie that has cute froggies in it. This will weaken your desire to exterminate the froggie.

Instead, keep telling yourself "If I don't get the frog, the frog will get me." Imagine yourself being attacked by a giant frog with a baseball bat.

5. Bring two burlap bags. One is for the frogs that look like lime Jell-O after you hit em with the bat. The other is for the frogs that keep jumpin around with permanent brain damage. Resist the temptation to club them repeatedly. Save them for boiling alive in hot water, where they die a long, slow, agonizing death similar to the early Catholic missionaries of Ecuador. This is half the fun of frogging.

6. After you've done this for a while, send $198.99 for a Joe Bob Briggs Industrial-Strength "Frog-Eater" Suction Device, with attached laser beam, that blinds the frog, paralyzes him, and then sucks him through a long metal tube that simultaneously rips his legs off for sale to area restaurants. The frog-giggin record, among those of us who swear by the Frog-Eater, is 17,498 frogs in a single night on a creek by the Arkansas River in Dardanelle, Arkansas. And let me point out that five bucks of the purchase price goes to the Fellowship of Christian Frog-Giggers, which sends out educational materials to people showing how we only do this to execute our God-given constitutional right to hunt for *sporting purposes only*.

Now, obviously, frogs are not the *only* things a young man will want to kill. But one reason boys never develop into *men* anymore is that these animal-rights fanatics think huntin is barbaric.

For example, I *love* to hunt turkeys, but I know I'm gonna get major flack from Wanda Bodine as soon as I whip out the old full-choke twelve-gauge, jump into a camouflage jumpsuit, and put on my hat with the little ear flaps.

For the last three, four years, Wanda's been on this animal-rights binge, which includes *turkeys*. Like they're not gonna die anyway! Like the zoos of America are gonna close because there aren't enough *turkeys* to look at!

I told her, "Wanda, there is nothing strange or perverted about blowing the head off a gobbler and splattering a little turkey flesh on a tree trunk. The whole country was founded on this principle. The Pilgrims did it."

But she won't listen. She thinks a human being with a twelve-gauge shotgun has an *advantage* over a turkey. And I've told her, "Wanda, there's more turkeys that escape than there are getting wasted. We only kill the stupid ones. It's important that the stupid turkeys die. Darwin said so."

But you can't use logic on this woman. So this year I'm gonna set down the complete rules and procedures of turkey hunting so that all you un-American Pilgrim-haters can understand.

1. We don't chase down the turkeys. No man could move that fast while luggin a beer chest. We sit in a hollowed-out tree log with bushes on our head, and we make a female turkey noise with a little reedy rubber gizmo that sounds like a fat man blowing his nose. If you're a male turkey, this sounds like a female turkey saying, "Hey, Rambo, wanna party?" When you hear a gobble, that means a tom turkey is answering back, "I'm gonna clean your transmission, honey"—and, as soon as he gets close to you, you unload both barrels of buckshot and watch him crumple to the earth and bleed to death. In other words, it's like working Times Square.

2. But let's say you don't want a tom turkey. You want a female. Most females are smarter than the males, so about the only ones you have a chance with are the jail-bait female turkeys,

the ones that were hatched this spring. You can buy a honker called a Kee Kee Run that will make em think they're going to an M. C. Hammer concert. Sometimes ten or twenty of em will run up to you together, like you're the New Kids on the Block's road manager. You can kill a lot more of these, because they're smaller. We professional turkey hunters call this the Roman Polanski Technique.

3. But the true turkey-hunting experts want to get old gobblers, the ones that are so old they don't mate anymore, and so you don't have a chance using the singles-bar line. They're just like human old people, though. All they wanna do is sit around and talk to other old turkeys and complain about their children. So what do you do? You make these *horrible* yelping sounds, which is what old gobblers sound like when they're whining, and this makes the elderly turkey think *you* are an elderly turkey, too, and so you *might* be willing to listen to him. You're making these noises that, to the turkey, sound like "Have I told you about my kidney problem?" And so they slowly wander over to you, but they're ornery. They don't trust you. You've got to keep talking forever—and it's worth it, because they're the biggest turkeys you can kill. And so you throw in stuff like "There hasn't been any decent music since Tommy Dorsey died" and "That Sid Caesar— now *there* was a comedian." And pretty soon the turkey comes over to bore you—only, as soon as he does, he gets three tons of shotgun pellets in his cute little elderly Mr. Grandpa Turkey face.

And Wanda thinks this is cruel to animals.
This is an *art form*.
Don't squelch this instinct in a young man. Let him flourish. Because, if he doesn't, he'll never move on to the next stage of male initiation—sittin around watching football on TV.

Spectator Spearing

As civilization advances, we can't always expect to live in rural areas where the killing of helpless inferior species is possible. So we've invented alternatives. The most popular one is, of course, rassling.

Do you realize there are still people in this world who believe rassling is fake?

I was in Orange County, California, a while back and got to talking with some professional yupsters who didn't see how people could get so worked up over rassling and fork over that much money to see the Junkyard Dog fight the Missing Link, specially people that had already graduated eighth grade. "I mean, even if they put on a great fight, what difference does it make who wins when the other one will probably win the next week?"

Now I'm gonna explain this once and for all for you rassling illiterates in the audience. I don't wanna have to do it again. Listen up.

You do *not* watch rassling to see who wins.

IRON JOE BOB

You watch rassling to see who *loses*.

Let's say we got two rasslers. One of em's name is Abdullah Roheimi, and the other one's name is Terry Leslie. You don't know nothin about either one. So the first week you go to the rassling matches to watch Abdullah Roheimi lose. Why? Cause you just flat out don't like the sound of his name.

You see the beauty here? In all the other parts of your life, you've got to have a reason to explain why you're not prejudiced. In rassling, you *never have to have a reason for anything*.

Okay, so Abdullah Roheimi comes out wearing a burnoose, Jesus sandals, and a big silver belt that says "Praise to Allah." Now you've got two reasons you wanna see Abdullah Roheimi get his face mashed in.

Next thing, Abdullah Roheimi shoves the referee for no reason. Up till now, you didn't care whether the referee got shoved or not. But you're in the grip of Rassling Fever. Abdullah Roheimi *can't do that*.

Okay, now Abdullah Roheimi is prancing around the ring like a sissy. He whips a little miniature American flag out of his hip pocket, and then he *eats it*. Reasons number four through ten to wanna see this guy get his hiney kicked to Lapland.

Now the rassling match starts. You haven't even *thought* about—what's his name again?—oh yeah, Terry Leslie. Just some guy in boxer shorts and a muscle shirt. But now all you care about is watchin' Terry Leslie beat the bejabbers out of this scum-guzzler Roheimi. But the match is delayed, while Roheimi calls time out. Why?

Because it's time to comb his beard and then pray to Mecca.

By the time he gets finished, Terry Leslie is complaining to the referee. So he's not looking behind him when Roheimi jumps off the top rope, scissor-kicks Terry Leslie to the back of the head, shoves him onto the concrete floor, jumps on his throat, grabs a folding chair out of the audience, and pounds Terry Leslie across the skull, drawing blood. Terry Leslie is being carried off on a stretcher, but before he goes, he requests the ring microphone.

"You're gonna *pay* for this," he says to Roheimi.

You get my drift here? Wouldn't *you* want tickets? Sooner or later the guy's gonna get it. Don't you wanna be there?

People say rassling is a battle of good and evil. Bullstuff. Rassling is the defeat of evil scum. We could care less about the good.

You understand this now?

Good.

But an even better example is the sport of baseball, where the American male is not only able to see good defeat evil scum, but is able to personally identify with every single player, even down to how much money they make and what their family problems are.

For example, I'm probly the only person you'll ever meet who has season tickets to the Texas Rangers baseball team. I think there are eight of us. There used to be more, but we lose two or three every year during the month of August when we start to realize that God didn't intend for baseball to be played in Texas. They just sort of keel over in their chairs, and a faint steamy mist rises up out of their skulls. We look out to the big thermometer on the right-field scoreboard and say, "Darn! We should of *known* Oscar was about to blow when it hit 112."

There are two kinds of games at Arlington Stadium, where the Rangers play. The first kind is a game where Nolan Ryan pitches. At these games there are 875,000 people in the stands, and you have to fight your way in because everybody's screaming stuff at you like "I'll give you five hundred dollars just to *touch* your ticket to this game!"

The other kind of game is . . . well . . . every other game the Rangers play. At these games, especially if it's a Tuesday night, there are 200 people in the stands, and you can actually have an influence on the outcome by yelling things at the batter like "Swing, you bozo!"

Actually, I don't think yelling "Swing, you bozo!" has ever worked, but when there are 200 people there, you have the *illusion* of affecting the outcome, which is just as good.

Anyhow, the problem of being a season ticket holder to the Texas Rangers is that we obviously need to come up with things to do during the actual games, and so mostly we talk about the players. We have to talk about *something,* or we'll end up eating the food. People who only go the ball game once a year can afford to devour steamy Velveeta nachos, the famous Super Dog, or ice cream served in a batting helmet, but it takes a four-day recovery period. Season ticket holders have to remain in top physical condition, because they're coming back tomorrow night.

Anyhow, in these group discussions, I usually have incisive analytical comments like "Pete Incaviglia doesn't look as fat this year."

But I've noticed in the last couple, three seasons that this just doesn't pass as legitimate baseball conversation anymore. You've gotta be able to say something like this:

"If Sierra doesn't increase his slugging percentage by another hundred points, he won't be able to win arbitration in the off season."

Or:

"Ever since Guzman had the arthroscopic on his elbow, his slider has slowed down."

(I should point out that I don't know whether it was Guzman or somebody else who "had the arthroscopic," and it might have been on his elbow or it might have been on his hiney for all I know, and I don't even know whether Guzman throws a slider. It's just an example.)

And my eyes glaze over.

Or they'll say:

"Rafael hasn't been hitting with power the last three weeks, but it's family problems."

Family problems?

It's *family* problems?

How do they know this?

The baseball fan of twenty years ago basically knew the names of the players on the team and in what order they batted. The players had no first names. "Did you see Carlton pitch yesterday? It was great!" This was about the level of conversation.

Then something happened. The devoted fan started calling these players by their first names. "Jeff is not concentrating tonight." Like you've just had a three-hour psychotherapy session with Jeff. Or "Ruben has got to get his temper under control." Like Ruben just came up in the stands and told you how much he hates the Orioles. And last names are only used when the player is in *big* trouble: "That Incaviglia stands *way* too far off the plate!"

But the truly amazing development is the amount of personal information the fan has about each player. "Well, you could almost predict José would have a bad year after he got that one-point-four-million contract."

They know the *exact* amount of money the guy makes, down to the "point-four." And there's always a little *resentment* about this, like, "If he was a *real* ball player, he wouldn't *care* so much about being a millionaire."

I don't know why sports fans are so bitter about players getting money, but they talk about it all the time, over and over and over again.

"You know, Mickey Mantle didn't earn in his whole career what that guy will make this one season."

"No player is worth that much money."

Like *they're* gonna get the money if the player doesn't.

Why do they feel so bitter about this? New Kids on the Block makes three million a week, but nobody goes to a New Kids on the Block concert and bitches about how much money they make. Larry Hagman got a couple hundred thou for every *episode* of *Dallas,* but nobody watched a scene of *Dallas* and then said, "Larry shouldn't have gotten the two hundred thou this week. That scene was *lame.*"

But ball players are *greedy.*

And they know about their *personal* lives.

"Well, his dad was an alcoholic, you know, and he was raised by his grandmother."

You're hearing this about a guy while you're watching him hit a ball with a bat and run around a field in his pajamas. And you wanna say, "You know what? I really didn't wanna know that. That's for, like, his priest or his shrink."

But, see, what's happening is they're exercising the old psychic Bronze Spear. Maybe they can't go turkey hunting anymore, but they can still watch Sierra swing for the fences. They're stuck in the Bronze Spear Phase. And their wives complain about it. But they have *no idea* what they're saying, because what follows the Bronze Spear Phase is a whole heck of a lot more dangerous than baseball.

You know what I'm talking about, don't you?

It's time to . . .

Dip the Dark Spear

B ack to the legend:

And the young boy, emboldened with the thrust of his rigid bronze spear, laid waste the countryside, until he was stopped one day at dusk by a Dark Princess who stole up behind him and cast a thick fishnet over his head. Strangely enough, the young boy didn't struggle, but allowed the Dark Princess to control him.

Recognize this one?

Think of it this way: "Would you like to buy me a drink, sailor?"

In other words, there's a period in the American male's life when he doesn't know exactly what to do with his spear, and so any woman who notices it, for any reason, can control it.

Let's get right to the point here: topless bars.

Have I ever told you about the time me and Phil Siegel and Fuzzy Nixon did the coast-to-coast topless-bar breast-o-rama?

It started out because Phil, who's from Brooklyn, claimed

that the Kit Kat Klub on Broadway in New York was the greatest topless bar in America. You could hear me and Fuzzy laughing all the way to Syracuse. The Kit Kat Klub, if you've ever been there, is the closest thing there is to watching grizzly bears take off their clothes for money. They got girls in there that have to be hosed down every five minutes just to keep the roaches off.

That's when Fuzzy Nixon, who's from Santa Monica, said the greatest go-go dancers in the world are at Oscar's nightclub in Anaheim. This is getting closer to the truth. But I insisted then, and I continue to insist today, that the greatest topless bar in the world is Baby Doll's Topless in the famous Bachman Lake "Hooter Heaven" area of Dallas, where—I'm just gazing at the newspaper here—this week the top two star attractions are Lulu Devine, billed as "the 8th and 9th Wonders of the World," and *Penthouse* centerfold girl Catalina Lamour. (Lulu's measurements, by the way, are billed as "85MM-23-34." I haven't gotten by there yet to verify those figures, but I will.)

Anyhow, it was shortly after that that Phil, Fuzzy, and me all gathered in New York and set out on a three-week cross-country topless-bar blitz that resulted in what I believe to be the only objective rankings of nekkid garbonzas ever compiled in one place. The results follow:

> **New York:** The only city in America where extinct buffalo breeds can be seen dancing topless. All the clubs are owned by guys named Khalil. All the girls look like junkie albinos.
>
> **New Jersey:** Same as New York, except the girls look like junkie albinos who live in the suburbs.
>
> **Boston:** Some *serious* sleaze. Dark bat caves where bug-eyed, frizzy-haired "exotic dancers" slide up and down a pole. Very weird. You've got to be a Yankee to be into it.

Florida: All the topless action is not in Miami, but in Tampa, the first place where some of the dancers assumed a vaguely humanoid form.

New Orleans: First city to go 100 percent transvestite on us. You have to be into Judy Garland.

Chicago: Fifty-five-year-old grandmas with cellulite. Women hired by Al Capone are *still* dancing. Very depressing.

Vancouver: Last city in North America where they have actual "burlesque" shows, like in *Flashdance*. Lots of leather and women named Cheree dancing to classical music. Interesting if you're casting a music video, but not erotic.

San Francisco: Broadway, where topless was founded by my close personal friend Carol Doda, better known as "The Twin Peaks" (long before the TV show ripped off her trademark), is pretty much down to two or three pathetic little clubs, mere shadows of the street's glory days. Carol is semiretired.

Vegas: They still wear balloons on their breasts and nine-foot peacock feathers on their heads, and if you ever see one of them close up, they all look like they had head-on collisions with a Max Factor truck.

El Lay: Oscar's in Anaheim has the "girl-next-door" type, but all the more famous places on the Sunset Strip are either closed or so sleazy your pocket gets picked before you even get out of your car. Porno stars will sell you their picture for five bucks at some of them. You *don't* wanna go inside.

Houston: The city where "table dancing" was invented (you have to see it to believe it) has decent-looking girls, and about 20 percent of them can actually dance.

Dallas: Still the topless bar capital of the world. Topless bars for every social class—Cabaret Royale for the high rollers, Million Dollar Saloon for the *nouveau riche,* and for the working man, the gritty Geno's Topless on Harry Hines Boulevard. These topless bars are so good that the local D.A. has declared them a public nuisance. And the most annoying one, for my money, is Baby Doll's—about thirty dancers all the time. They got girls in that place that look good *before* the third beer, and, of course, that's the highest compliment I can pay to a woman.

Now.

That was at least ten years ago that we did the cross-country breast-o-rama, and ever since then there has been an *explosion* in American topless. Am I the only one that's noticed this, or did somebody build about *nine thousand* new topless bars in this country just last year?

I guess it's not *that* strange, when you realize that *two million* women have gotten silicone breast implants. After all, once you've gone to the trouble to get em, what are you gonna do, just stare in the mirror all day? You might need some independent verification.

But what's interesting about this particular trend is that they don't call em "topless bars" anymore. They're "gentlemen's clubs." A lot of em even have *dress codes.*

When I was growing up, the only things they checked you for at the door was a) beer and b) firearms. Anything else on your body could be brought into the club.

Do you realize you can eat a buffet lunch every day for *free* at most topless . . . er . . . gentlemen's clubs in major American cities? I'm not kidding. You walk into the club, *grab a plate,* and the announcer says, "Our next dancer is the lovely Tawnee—and how about those *ribs* today, gentlemen?"

And everything else inside these clubs is a million-dollar

investment, too. I can remember when the only drinks they sold in topless bars were beer, whiskey, whiskey-and-Coke, and, in case you were on a diet, Jack-Daniel's-and-Diet-Dr.-Pepper. (I'm from Texas.)

Oh yeah, there *was* one more: the kamikaze. I don't know if topless bars *invented* kamikazes, but they certainly perfected the most efficient *use* of kamikazes. After the guys sit through the last lame dance by the last plug-ugly dancer, they start thinking, "Well, nothing left to see here. There's *another* night of my life *wasted* because I'm a pathetic loser weenie. Guess I'll go get the pickup and head to the house." And what magic sound do they hear?

"Gentlemen, for the next five minutes only, all kamikazes are *on the house!* Please welcome the gorgeous Juuuuuleeeeee. . . ."

And Juuuuuleeeeee would, of course, be the only decent-looking stripper they had in the place. And she looked *especially* good at the *end* of that kamikaze.

What's in those things anyhow?

What got me thinking about this is that recently an old boy from Fort Worth named Don Waitt sent me his pride and joy, a fat 182-page annual directory called *Exotic Dancer* that lists every strip joint in the country. Actually, it sorts them out into the following categories:

Nude Bars
Topless Bars
Gentlemen's Clubs
Stripper Clubs
Go-Go Bars

Whew! When did it get so dang complicated? Here's the difference, according to Don:

"Nude" means the dancers get nekkid as mud-weasels.

"Topless" means they get nekkid as . . . Why am I explaining this? Topless means topless.

Now it gets complicated: "Go-go," according to the book, "can mean bikinis, lingerie, pasties and T-backs or G-strings, and in some cases simply shorts and halters. It all depends on local city ordinances."

Are you like me? Are you thinking, at this very moment, "T-back? T-back? I should know what that is, shouldn't I? Gosh, I hope I don't have to *ask* somebody." . . . On second thought, I might not wanna know.

I don't know about "Stripper Clubs." I looked through the book, and I think it's those places that have fifty-five-year-old women with faces like sides of pork loin, dancing with a lot of feather boas and working with snakes and stuff. They used to have em at the Arkansas State Fair. This lean cancerous guy would stand outside the tent and say, "This show is *not for kiddies.* If you want a *kiddie show,* move *right on down the midway,* there's a ride down there that goes up and down, up and down, *no sir, this is adult entertainment, adults only,* featuring some of the most beautiful women in the world doing things that might *shock* you. . . ." And they *would* shock you, because you wanna yell "Put your goldurn clothes *back on.* That cellulite is *disgusting."*

Anyhow, my point is that topless bars are bigger and fancier than ever. There's even one that advertises in *The New York Times* every day. They've got a topless bar in Atlanta that has fifty women onstage at the same time. They've got all kinds of special promotions like "go-go-ramas," amateur nights, bachelor parties, the beloved wet T-shirt contest (invented in the seventies and still going strong), "table dancing," "couch dancing," "bar dancing," "lap dancing" (don't ask). And when you really think about it, and you really wonder what all this explosion of jiggly flesh means, you've got to admit:

We American men have become a nation of *watchers*, haven't we?

If this is what we're doing—or a large number of us are doing it—then we're obviously confused about just *who* has the interests of our Bronze Spear at heart.

Lemme give you a hint:

It's not the gorgeous Julie.

That's all I'm gonna say.

Think about it.

Dragging Your Spear in the Toxic Muck

ll right, where are we?

Oh yeah, drunk at a topless bar.

Okay, I think this would be a good place to ask the question, "How did we end up drunk at a topless bar?"

Easy.

Modern civilization *hates* it when we exercise the Bronze Spear. Everything is stacked against us. Nobody wants us to be hanging out with the Dark Princess in the first place.

For example, there's this bar on the beach in Capitola, California, where you're not allowed to buy a three-quart permanent-brain-damage El Tequila Grande margarita anymore, even though when I made my annual trip to San Francisco last year, these buddies of mine in Daly City drove me down to Capitola just especially to witness and behold the three-quart permanent-brain-damage El Tequila Grande margarita. I started out having the *frozen* three-quart et cetera margarita, but after one of those I couldn't actually lift the second one, so I canned the ice and only had six, seven more of em before we left. It had no effect on me whatsoever. I drove us back up the coast to San Francisco, and we even had enough energy to stop in Vegas for a meal.

Now the reason why you can't buy the El Tequila Grande anymore is because of something they're calling "responsible beverage service." And you know what my favorite part of "responsible beverage service" is?

The waitress doesn't bring you your drink when you ask for it. She hangs around in the back—*on purpose.*

In my opinion this is enough reason to shut down California and move the whole state out to Texas where we still pour doubles, triples, and octuples, for that matter, without any weenie-ing around.

Another thing they're doing now in California is not serving beer by the pitcher. Do you realize what this would do to the state of Texas if the idea spread? Do you realize the effect that one thing has on the life of poor people who can't afford to pay for ten beers by the *single?* Do you realize the number of people that would have to do all their drinking in Mexico just to quench their thirst?

Not only that, I found out this bar in Capitola is getting *federal* money for this business. *My* money, which I shell out every time I buy a fifth of Jack Daniel's or a keg of Bud. They call this a "luxury tax" even though you wouldn't think so if you went into Bobo's Barb-Wire Museum and Lounge on Highway 67. If the guys in there didn't drink beer by the pitcher, they wouldn't get any nutrition at all.

Anyhow, I was in Bobo's place the other night pouring some Triple Sec shooters down my throat for medicinal purposes, when Bobo started talking about how he practices "responsible beverage service" himself.

"When a guy comes in from California," he said, "I ask him if he wants a Texas Super Loco."

"And what's that?" I asked Bobo.

"A jigger of lime juice, a thimble of tequila, three teaspoons of Bartles and Jaymes." Bobo paused a minute for dramatic effect. "And three quarts of water."

I told him I thought that was a good idea if he didn't want one of those California guys to report him to the Responsible Beverage Society.

"Besides," Bobo said, "it makes em feel at home."

Isn't it sick, that this could happen in America? Believe me, it's Bronze Spear haters.

Another example of ways they try to confuse you, throw you off balance:

Have you noticed how, every time you go in a restaurant these days, some loony in a painter's smock comes out carrying a five-foot-long marital aid full of pepper and asks you if he can grind some of it out on your food?

How did this tradition get started?

If this is so important to your food, how come nobody did it till about ten years ago?

"Would you like some *fresh* pepper?" the guy says, and he's pointing this Scud missile at your plate. The thing is so big he's got it mounted on his shoulder like a bazooka.

He always says this when you've just got your salad and you're holding the *normal* pepper in your hand. What are you supposed to say?

"No, thank you, I prefer this groady *stale* pepper in the little plastic bottle that looks like it's been sitting here since *My Three Sons* went off the air."

So what you're *really* thinking is, "Do I even *want* pepper on this food? What is this blackened monkfish elephant sauté gunk gonna taste like anyhow? It *looks* like it will taste like a Goodyear tire. If I put pepper on it, it might just taste like a Goodyear tire with pepper on it. And even if it *doesn't* taste like a Goodyear tire, the *pepper* might taste like a Goodyear tire, and so there's way too many decisions to make about it right now while I've got my fork poised in attack position."

So this is what you *should* say, but what do you *really* say?

"Oh, yes, fresh pepper, mmmmmmmm, can't wait."

And this is what the guy's waiting for. He goes into this Nigerian belly dance with a lot of elbow action while he grinds that stuff out and circles your plate like he's dumping rat repellent around a donut, and then, after he's put two quarts of pepper on top of your gabardine endive tartare or whatever it is, he says, "Say when!"

And you go "When! When!" Like "Why didn't you *tell* me it was *my* decision? I thought you were putting the *proper* amount of pepper on a piece of veal sauterne à la Palermo, because you're the *expert* who brought this Pakistani birth-control device over to my table *in the first place!*"

But by that time it's too late, because you have this three-inch Mount McKinley of pepper sitting on your arugula, and it's in these *one-pound chunks!* This is some kind of pepper that has to be chiseled out of a mine in Venezuela. There are teenagers coming by the table and spray-painting graffiti on the sides of your pepper chunks.

And you're thinking, *"I didn't even want pepper!"*

The other day this happened to me for about the ten millionth time, and I turned to Wanda Bodine and I screamed at her: "What the hell *is* pepper anyhow? And why do I need it?"

And she said, "I don't know. I think it's some kind of flower that they grind up."

And I said, "You're telling me I'm putting mutilated flowers on my food?"

And she said, "I don't know. You should look it up in the encyclopedia."

And I said, "I don't *want* to look it up in the encyclopedia, I just want to eat my teriyaki burrito and go home."

And the guy in the Betty Crocker valet parker's uniform came back over and said, "Is something wrong?"

And I said, "Yeah, you put too much pepper on my gazpacho lotus roll."

And he said, "I'm sorry."

And I said, "Don't let it happen again. If you're gonna ask me to say when, then ask me to say when *before* you start dumping charcoal briquets on my food, okay?"

And he said, "I didn't realize."

And I said, "It's okay."

And he said, "There will be no charge."

And I said, "It's okay. I'll pay for all the mutilated flowers I ate. I'm just putting you on notice that I'm *taking control of my life,* okay?"

And he said, "I understand."

And he did.

Sorry I got off on that. What was I talking about?

Oh yeah—reasons that you can't just go probing the countryside with your Bronze Spear anymore. See, there used to be *established ways* to become male. But now, nobody knows *what* it means. And we keep getting these scientific reports that say the whole idea of *macho* might just be some kind of thing in your DNA or your hormones or whatever. This doctor in La Jolla, California, has found the part of your brain that makes you a homosexual. It's called the anterior hypothalamus, and it's basically the size of a mosquito's toe.

Actually, I'm saying it wrong. If you're a heterosexual, it's the size of a mosquito's toe. If you're a homosexual or a woman, it's the size of a gnat's toenail.

In other words, the bigger the hypothalamus, the more your

brain sends out signals like "Get a load of the hematomas on that one!" And the *smaller* the hypothalamus, the more likely you're gonna be thinking "Do my shoes match my purse?" or "I just *love* Julie Andrews in *The Sound of Music.*" And there's *nothing* you can do about it.

This makes perfect sense to me, except I can already see problems, now that we know this. For one thing, guys are gonna be calling up brain surgeons demanding to have their hypothalami measured. And then we'll do brain scans and find out that Warren Beatty has a hypothalamus the size of a hippopotamus, but Harvey Fierstein's hypothalamus looks like a smudge of vegetable soup on the linoleum. And the guys with the well-developed hypothalami will start having X-ray pictures taken and advertising in magazines:

> With a brain stem like this, I'll *never* get sick of having sex with you. Call 970-HYPO.
>
> Wanna pick my brain? It's a handful!
>
> Do you like long walks in the park? So do I. That's because, as you can see, my hypothalamus is so un-developed that I'd rather walk around talking than have sex. Look how small it is. We could get married and you could manipulate me for the rest of your life.

You see what I'm talking about?

There's another problem here, though, because this same doctor says that the hypothalamus is formed while you're still a fetus, so it's something the parents could argue about later.

"You just *had* to have a pack of Winstons that night you were pregnant with little Timmy. I'm telling you, the boy's *not right.*"

"It's just a stage. A lot of little boys dress up in women's clothes."

"The kid is fourteen and he's dressing up like Marilyn Chambers! I don't think so!"

"Well, it must be something from *your* hillbilly gene pool then!"

Then you've got the matter of defense attorneys.

"Your Honor, there's a perfectly good reason why my client would rape three hundred and seventy women in a three-day period. Look at the size of this hypothalamus."

And the judge would have to say, "Well, if he can't control it, he needs to have a hypothalamotomy."

And then you would have mental hospitals all over the country opening up brain stems so you could bring the hypothalamus down to the level of "acceptable community standards."

Actually, the more I think about it, the more I hope the guy's a quack. Because, let's face it, if your hypothalamus can control you that much, then we're not *human beings,* we're *machines* that can be *manipulated* by our mere biological needs and every time we think of a blond bimbo wearing tight Spandex and spiked high heels, or stuffing herself into one of those underwire support bras, or . . . I gotta hurry up and finish this chapter.

The Fear of Losing Your Spear

When we last looked in on him, our young brave was entangled in fishnet. Now you might be wondering why he couldn't just rip through the fishnet with the sword. Think about that for a minute. Study the fishnet on the stocking of a forty-dollar hooker.

I rest my case.

The fact is, most guys would *never* leave the net of the Dark Princess if they didn't have to. But there comes a point in your life when a great thundering noise calls to you from the distance, and you move on. It usually sounds like this:

"Get off your lazy butt and get a job!"

(The precise wording might vary according to your neighborhood.)

And part of the reason we have such trouble going forward from here is that we don't really *want* to grow up. We *hate* the word *old*. And so we get to be fifty-five years old and we're still trying to fix up the Chevy because "I might wanna race it at Daytona someday."

IRON JOE BOB

It used to be just women that had this problem, but now I think men are a lot worse. Remember last year when everybody started treating George Foreman and Nolan Ryan like they were the Great Hopes of Future Ages because they were still doing amazing athletic feats after the age of forty? After all, if Nolan can throw a no-hitter when he's forty-four years old, then maybe I can start training for the Metropolitan Opera. Who *says* you can't start learning *The Barber of Seville* when you're forty-five? This is the *nineties*. This is *America*. This is the Age of No Age.

You notice how nobody uses the word "middle-aged" anymore? You call somebody "middle-aged," it's about like saying "You have a face like a constipated moose." One night on *The Tonight Show* Johnny Carson told Buddy Hackett he should think of himself as "middle-aged."

"If I'm middle-aged," Buddy said, "where are all the hundred-and-twenty-year-old people?"

We used to have "over the hill" parties when people turned thirty, or forty, or fifty, or whatever. This used to be a source of *amusement*. When my grandpa retired, his buddies at the phone company gave him joke gifts like walking sticks and knitting needles.

Now, all of a sudden, you can't tell these jokes anymore.

"Well, I'm forty-eight, but I *feel* twenty-eight."

Since when am I supposed to care how old you *feel?*

"All the people in my family are long-lived. Two of my grandmothers lived into their early nineties."

Yeah, so what does this have to do with how old you are?

Lemme explain something here. How old you are is a *mathematical fact.* It's not negotiable. You start with the day you were born, and you count all the days and months and years until you get to today, and that's *how old you are.* Am I getting this across? It's a number. That's the *only* number of your age. You can't think about it real hard and make it a *different number.*

Is this clear?

You ever notice how, about the age of thirty-five, people start going crazy with the exercise routines? Firm up, slim down, pump iron, run laps. And a lot of em I understand—they *feel* bad, and so they wanna feel *better*. Or they're athletes or dancers or actors, and if they don't pump up their deltoids, they'll lose their jobs. But there's also a lot of people who are doing this stuff because of some vague reason like "I believe in exercise."

You what?

I can understand "I believe in God," "I believe in the First Amendment," or even "I believe in premarital sex." But who can *believe* in exercise? It's like, no matter what you look like or feel like, or what you're trying to do with your life, you want to exercise for the *sake* of exercise. It's a Zen thing. It's like you wouldn't be a decent human being if you didn't do it.

So all these Ponce de Leóns are out there working that Stairmaster, jerking those free weights, playing the sadistic game of racquetball because they believe there's gonna be some reward when they get through. They're gonna be forty-eight and look twenty-eight. Of course, you could save all that time by going the plastic surgery route, but that would be too easy. They wanna do it the Old Testament way. They want fiery trials and ordeals. They wanna trudge forty years through the desert, fighting off middle age, retirement age, and old age. They wanna be immortal.

Fortunately, a new study came out last year proving just how immortal we can be. It has a graph showing the difference in life-style between a person in top physical condition and a person who never gets any exercise. At the age of twenty they're equally healthy. By the age of forty the lazy guy is able to do just a little less. At the age of sixty the difference is slightly greater. At the age of eighty, the lazy guy might have to stay indoors. The exercising guy will get to keep going out until he's eighty-eight. (Of course, by this time, he's spent eight years of his life jogging.)

But the most interesting part of the study involved the question Who will die first?

God threw em a curve ball.

If everything else is equal, and the only difference between these two guys is that one exercises and one doesn't, they'll die at exactly the same time.

I find this very, very amusing.

Anyhow, my point was that women have had this thing about staying young for a long time, but men have only started getting really paranoid about it during the last twenty years. I think it got especially bad when Reagan was president, because the guy kept getting these disgusting *male* diseases. Every five minutes, some reporter was turning in a new article about Ronnie's gizzards. It was gross stuff, too. If I said that stuff at the dinner table, my mama would slap me nekkid. I got to where I wouldn't pick up the paper until I had it dusted for "polyp removal" and—most terrifying of all—"colon flushing."

Why couldn't he have had some *decent* disease, like permanent brain damage? The Bethesda Naval Hospital kept hauling him in to be cleaned up, emptied out, flushed, drained, lanced, and sucked dry, but *I don't wanna hear about it!* Is that understood? Right here is a list of *exactly* what I don't wanna hear about:

1. I do *not* want any descriptions of how they inserted a tube with "an electrified loop" through Ronnie's "urethra" to "scrape away the enlarged prostate tissue." This sounds like they bent a coat hanger, held it over a match, and said, "Close your eyes now, Mr. President."

2. I do *not* want to know about his "colonoscopy." I don't know what a colonoscopy is, but it sounds like something very slimy that drips.

3. I do *not* want to hear about "intestinal polyps" that *grow*.

4. I do *not* want to hear about "the two feet of large intestine removed by doctors in 1985." How come every single one of these articles had to talk about "the two feet of large intestine removed by doctors in 1985"? Listen to me: It's *gone*. It's *dead*. We *can't get it back*. It went in the garbage disposal! Stop talkin about it. Forget it. He can *use what he's got*.

5. I do *not* want to hear about how all Ronnie's disgusting problems are "common to older men." We do *not* have to think about this until our own gizzards get gummed up. We do *not* have to know this is gonna happen to us. We can *eat what we want*.

   So stop it. Just stop it.

Sorry I got a little carried away there, but you start to get paranoid about these things. And now we've got a new one. Every doctor in America is handing out these little pamphlets that strike fear into the hearts of men throughout the land. Remember when breast exams became such a big deal in the eighties, and there were free breast-exam clinics, and movies about breast cancer, and TV shows where they talked about breast self-examination, and I even helped out the American Cancer Society in my syndicated newspaper column by recognizing Breast Awareness Week. Of course, *every* week for me is Breast Awareness Week, but I meant well.

So now we have the *male* version of breast awareness. And it's called . . . oh my God, this is gonna be tough . . . it's called "testicular self-examination." Just the *sound* of it makes me wanna bend over like a rhesus monkey and hop around in pain.

But it's true. Next time you guys go to the doctor—which in Texas normally means once a year when you get your gunshot wound—you're gonna find out about this. You've *got* to do it. They scare the bejabbers out of you, telling you how this testicular cancer—can we *please* get a new name for this?—how it sneaks up on you even when you're young.

And so you just about get over the shock of hearing the doctor say the word *testicles* about thirty times, and then he tells you you're gonna have to do this "procedure" to yourself once a month. And you're going, "Yeah, okay, fine, I can live with this." And then he tells you *what the procedure is!*

And you go *"Yeeeeeeeeooooooowwwwwwwww!"* and double over in his office like a man who's just been rammed through the stomach with a fire poker.

But they know you're gonna react like this. They're ready for you. So then they tell you *why* you *have* to do it: because if you don't do it you might not be able to have children. And this gets to some guys, scares em. Others go, "Can you *give* me this disease immediately?"

Then they tell you you might also lose all your facial hair. Not pleasant, but, after all, we've got your Hair Club for Men, we've got your Kojak look, we've got your J. C. Penney toupee.

Then they tell you that if you're not alert for testicular cancer, you might end up with a voice like Goldie Hawn.

And that's probly enough to turn the tables right there, because unless you want a lifetime career as a professional weatherman, I don't think most men could handle the voice thing.

But then they clobber you with the biggie:

If you get this disease, you might grow *breasts*. You know, big ones, like those guys on Forty-second Street.

And so pretty soon you're saying, "Can I have, like, *fifty* of those brochures, in case I lose the first forty-nine and forget how to do my monthly testicular self-examination?"

But to answer your main question, guys:

Yes, you feel like a *complete idiot* when you do it.
I know. I hate it.
But I also don't have breasts.
How did I get off on that?
I have *got* to start staying on the subject.

Does My Spear Look Funny to You?

I better get back to the Indian legend, or else you'll think I'm just making this stuff up as I go along.

> *At length the young brave, sated with darkness, feeling the life sucked out of him, saw the sun beginning to rise—and at that moment he saw the Dark Princess fully revealed: a withered hag, leering at him like Death. He shrunk back in terror, cried out, and fled into the enchanted forest. But everywhere he looked he saw strange shapes, phantasms, ghosts, and apparitions. He knew not where he was.*

Don't you hate it when you see em without their makeup on?

Anyhow, we've gotta face it. There comes a time in your life when you don't know *what* you are. Everybody treats you like an alien. Everybody acts like your life is screwed up. Out of nowhere, for no reason, people will say things like "Nice shirt." And you look down at the shirt you've been wearing three times a week for fifteen years, and you say to yourself, "That's funny. Nobody's ever noticed it before."

All of a sudden the rules are all changed. And you're the only guy who doesn't know what they are.

It especially happens to single guys.

In fact, you know what the great new wave of bigotry is gonna be. I can see it coming now. It's too late to stop it. What person in America is soon to become more abused than the smoker, more passé than a Jimmy Carter liberal, more *out of it* than a cocaine user with gold neck chains at Studio 54?

The person with no children.

More important, the person who doesn't want to *talk* about his children.

It starts when people move out of your neighborhood and talk to you like it's a *moral* decision.

"It's been nice knowing you, Joe Bob, but now that little Wilhelmina is on the way, we've decided to move to a town that's a *better place for kids to grow up.*"

And you're going "What? Is there something I don't know about the neighborhood?"

And they say, "You know, a place that's *quieter,* more laid back."

And you try to talk to em, by saying something sensible like "Roger, I've never known a child in my *life* that liked *quiet* places. Every child I ever met liked fireworks, baseball games, carnivals, subway rides, video arcades, hundreds of people, mud pies, and *chaos.*"

"Well, you're entitled to your opinion."

There's this *thing* that comes over people when they have babies—no, even *before* they have babies. They don't want any of you *irresponsible* childless people even *breathing* on the *fetus.*

"Besides," says Roger, "we could never send Wilhelmina to school here. We've got to find a decent school district."

And perhaps you say something like, "Rog, we're dealing with a three-week-old fetus here that's about the size of an Egg McMuffin. I don't think you need to worry about what calculus teacher they're hiring this year."

And they get so *miffed*, because, see, you're *taking this too lightly*.

"It might surprise you to know that I want the very *best* education for this child," Rog will say. He always tells me "it might surprise you to know" things that it never surprises me to know.

It comes down to this: once a person has a child, or even has the *prospect* of having a child, or even *decides* to have a child, he becomes a different species from the rest of humanity.

He orders the Lifetime Network. He re-ups his subscription to *National Geographic*. He starts talking about cholesterol and how, after the kid is born, they won't be eating at McDonald's anymore, because they don't want the kid to get "hooked" on that stuff.

"Hey, Rog, what if it works the same way as crack babies? The kid will be *born* addicted to McDonald's."

Rog doesn't think this is funny.

And they all enroll in some kind of secret psychology class and start using words like "setting a good example" and "providing an environment that encourages freedom" and "displaying love as a healthy emotion."

And after a while you have to say, "Rog, are you studying to be a priest or *what?*"

Whatever happened to buying the kid a baseball bat?

It gets worse after the kid is born. Ask Rog and Elaine to come over and watch a little TV on the weekend.

"Naw, with the baby, we just can't pick up and go like that."

"Go ahead, bring the baby. I like babies."

"It's not that easy. We've got all the diaper stuff, and she's got these nap times, and it's—"

"Rog! I've got places the baby can *sleep!* I've got *room deodorizer!* It's *no problem!*"

"Well, yeah, thanks, but, naw, not today."

Because evidently it would be like traveling to another planet. The planet of the Childless. The planet of the people who *never grew up* and had children of their own. The people that sometimes still go eat dinner at ten o'clock at night and do other irresponsible things like *drive their cars too fast* when there are *children,* strapped into their little car-carriers, *traveling on that same road.* The people that just *don't understand.* The *scum.* The *lazy people.* The *selfish* people. The people that only think about themselves and *can't stand the grown-up responsibility* of being fathers and mothers.

And so after a while—after a few years of this—after you think you've lost these people as friends forever, suddenly you make a *new* friend. Their baby is now six years old, and he wants *out* of the house. He starts visiting you, and he's *more interesting* than his daddy. He doesn't wanna talk about cholesterol. He wants to play football and root around in the dirt and visit the *neat part of town* where you live, instead of the boring part of town where his parents live. In other words, he's become exactly what his daddy was before he experienced the miracle and the joy of childbirth.

So, if you are one of the Ostracized, just hang around. Your new buddy will show up any day now.

But there are lots more ways the modern world makes us feel like aliens. For example, if you pay any attention to the media at all, you'll eventually decide that a) you don't have sex enough, b) you don't know *how* to have sex correctly, and c) everyone else knows more about sex than you do.

Here's an example of what I mean.

On the same day, in America, in the year 1991, the following news events occurred:

1. Geraldo Rivera published an "I Was a Sex Pig" book revealing all the women he supposedly diddled around with.

2. *Vanity Fair* published an interview with Jessica Lange in which she goes on and on about all the sexual aardvarking she was doing with Sam Shepard at the same time she was carrying on "a European relationship" (whatever that is) with Mikhail Baryshnikov.

3. A woman named Tai Collins, "Miss USA Virginia 1983," held a press conference in Washington, D.C., where she unveiled her *Playboy* magazine photo layout and described the hanky-panky that supposedly went on in a room at the Hotel Pierre in New York City with Senator Charles Robb, who happens to be married to the daughter of an ex-president.

4. Mickey Rourke agreed to give an interview to *The Village Voice,* on the condition that he could be asked about anything *except* his relationship with a woman named Carre Otis. I have no idea who Carre Otis is, but if I were to see Mickey on the street, I'd want to roll down my window and scream out, "Hey, Mickey! I know *all about* Carre!"

5. Actor Alec Baldwin was photographed at the U.S. Open tennis tournament sitting next to superstar Monica Seles. When a CBS reporter interviewed Monica a few minutes later, she asked her, "When will you be seeing Alec again?" Monica had no clear-cut answer.

Do we really need to know all this stuff?

Did I miss something, or did Robin Leach recently become the president of every single media organization in America?

Somehow I don't think these are the same news stories being reported by the media in Lithuania.

I have a theory about how it got this way, though, and it goes like this:

1776: "All men are created equal."

1865: "All men are created equal. We really mean it this time."

1917: "All men are created equal, and we even mean women, too."

1946: "All men are entitled to their own opinion."

1964: "The votes of all men are equal."

1967: "The opinions of all men are equal."

1969: "The opinions of all men are correct, each in his own way."

1973: "All men are entitled to all the information about their government."

1976: "All men are entitled to all the information about their government and their politicians and anybody running for office."

1980: "All men are entitled to know everything about anybody who's running for office, in office, or just a big shot."

1984: "All men are entitled to know everything about anybody who's rich."

1987: "All men are entitled to know everything about anybody who's a movie star or athlete or anything else where it seems like they're getting way too much money for whatever feeble thing it is that they do."

1991: "All men are entitled to know everything about everybody."

I think you can see where this has led us. It has led us straight into the dark recesses of Geraldo Rivera's bedroom.

Freedom can be *very* scary.

So you feel like an alien in your own neighborhood, a misfit in your own bedroom—but the main place *none* of us fits in anymore is with our families. Do you realize we have more homicides per American household on Thanksgiving Day than any other day of the year?

You might be saying "Is that so?" But you are *not* saying "I don't believe it." Are you?

One theory I have about why people start getting depressed and thinking about *death* around the holidays is cranberry sauce. We all hate cranberry sauce. The only people that like cranberry sauce are named Estelle. Eleven months of the year we don't even have to *think* about cranberry sauce. And then what happens?

Jigglin purple igloos sloshed on your plate.

People see that, they just go crazy, start killin the in-laws.

Another reason: people walkin around the house wearin house shoes that look like mooseheads. This wouldn't be pleasant even if your relatives looked like the Radio City Rockettes, but since your relatives probly *don't* look like the Radio City Rockettes, since they probly look more like the night shift at Dunkin' Donuts, then this is like watching a coffee-table leg model underwear.

That's why I've come up with a few commonsense rules for getting through the holiday season without a) dying, b) serving twenty to life, or c) mutilating a pet. Listen up, I don't wanna have to tell you this stuff again.

1. *Conversation:* Never start out a conversation with somethin' like "I *told* her she never should of married that Jimmy Bohannon." Try something like this: "Loretta and them moved to Waco." Don't add anything to it. Stop right there. Don't say: "Loretta and them moved to Waco, she's so *nice.*" This starts an argument about how nice she is.

2. *Food:* Never ask who made what unless *you already know the answer.* Never say "Who made the marshmallow jelly-bean fruit salad?" unless you're sure the marshmallow jelly-bean fruit salad is a) *all gone* and b) nobody scraped it off into the garbage disposal.

3. *Football:* Never ask any embarrassing questions about the game, like "Who's playing?" or "What's the score?" unless you're sure all the old men in the room are *awake.* Just remember this: it's always the most important game of the year. If it wasn't, then you'd all be in there clearing off the table.

4. *Presents:* When you open it up, *never* state what it is while you're opening it. Just say "That's so *niiiiiiiice! Thaaaaaaaaank yoooooouuuuu!"* And then figure out what it is later. Also, as soon as you get out of sight of the house, *destroy* all bottles of men's cologne so you won't be tempted to throw it in the drawer at home with all the forty-eight other bottles you got at other holidays, cause someday you just might go over the Jade East limit and send a dear beloved family member a bomb in the mail.

5. *Divorces:* Anybody that was there last year but not this year *does not exist.* Always remember this. Your life could depend on it.

This is getting depressing. Let's move on.

Cappuccino My Butt

Speaking of modern stuff that ticks me off but I can't figure out what chapter to put it in, aren't you sick of these places at the mall that sell Guatemalan cinnamon-root coffee beans?

You know the places that have the little Japanese ceramic mugs at the back with pictures of spindly cherry trees on em, and automatic coffeemakers from Germany that cost nine hundred bucks? Because, after all, if you're gonna drink a thirty-two-dollar bag of Nairobi Aroma Black Beetle Cappuccino Mix, then obviously you've got to own a giant chrome Brewmaster that looks like a life-support machine, and you've got to *drink* that liquid giraffe juice out of a mug that weighs seven pounds and reflects your entire kitchen in its glistening cobalt surface.

You know what I'm talking about? When did this coffee thing happen? Wasn't it about ten years ago that everybody decided they *hated* coffee? Remember? What became the universal after-dinner cry of the yuppie?

"Do you have decaf?"

So when did everybody go from thinking coffee-drinking was a form of herpes to this new idea that a fourteen-dollar cup of Tahitian Vanilla-Wombat Espresso will turn you into an art director for music videos?

It's the truth. They even have interior designers come in and paint the tables and walls so you'll *feel* just exactly right when you raise your pinky and tip that gusher of Maltese Master Blend into your happy gullet.

Of course, if you make a whole pot of the stuff, you'll also need to buy a Scandinavian coffee strainer and a Turkish coffee thermos, because only *rednecks* would let the goldurn coffee sit there in the coffeemaker for more than thirty seconds, losing its "aroma de dirty sock."

Actually, I think I know who's behind this deal. Look around these Shoppes de Café in the malls and see what the most expensive items for sale are. That's right: pottery.

Mug makers.

Pot makers.

Fat women in Birkenstock sandals who live in Colorado. That's who's behind it. They know what they're doing. Don't trust em.

Remember, it only takes one coffee-swilling bug-eyed high-strung yuppie to feed thirty-seven bovine potters per year. Don't add to the problem. Boycott foreign coffee. Maxwell House'll do just fine.

Thank you for letting me get that off my chest. Now back to our story.

The Twisted Spear

When the Krankaway Indian guru tells us that the young brave "knew not where he was," what's he really trying to say, in modern terms?

He's screwed up.

He's twisted.

He's weirded out. Right?

Because what do you have to be in America, in the nineties, to be considered truly grown-up? What do you need to be a man?

You need at least one good old-fashioned addiction.

The Modern Confession. It goes something like this:

I repent of smoking cigarettes. It was cool when I started, but it became uncool and I quit. It was hard. I was an addict. I was a miserable nicotine-head, two packs of Marlboros a day, but I quit, and I'm proud that I quit.

Unfortunately, it was the seventies, so I became a cokehead. Remember when it was cool to snort powder? It *was*. It really *was*. That's the only reason I did it. But I became a sniveling paranoid cocaine addict, and so I got professional help. And I quit. It was hard. I was an addict, but I quit. I'm proud that I quit.

Unfortunately, it was so hard quitting cocaine that I started smoking cigarettes again. But this time I only smoked *one* pack of Marlboros a day, and I was proud of that. But I could see after a while that I was only fooling myself, and so I quit.

Unfortunately, I started drinking more and more. First it was two or three scotches at lunch, then it was seven or eight scotches at dinner, and finally it was seventeen scotches, seven tequila shooters, nine vodka martinis, and a Coco Loco for breakfast. For a long time I told myself I could control it, but the day came when I had to face the fact that I was an addict. I was a miserable smelly drunk, and I had to quit. So I quit.

Then, after six months of quitting, I got real drunk one night and quit again. I was real proud of quitting, especially the second time.

Unfortunately, when I was coming off the liquor, I got addicted to coffee. My shrink said it was this oral fixation that I have. Sometimes I would drink ninety-four cups a day. It was affecting my stomach, my complexion, and my eyeballs were turning green. It took courage to admit that I needed help, but I finally sought caffeine-addiction counseling, and eventually I was able to quit.

It was about three months later that I realized how fat I was getting. I loved chocolate. And I loved food in general. I would go to Denny's in the middle of the afternoon and eat the whole left side of the menu, then I would go to Mrs. Field's Cookies for dessert. One week I gained thirty pounds. People thought I was dying of cancer. They thought it was medication that was bloating my body. I took down all the mirrors in the house because I didn't want to see the truth—I had become a four-hundred-and-seventy-pound circus freak. I tried Ultra Slim Fast for a while, but I was able to drink nine hundred and fifty milkshakes a day, so that didn't work. Finally, I went to obesity camp, where they chain you to a bed, wire your jaws shut, and beat the crap out of you every time you mention food. After three months of therapy, I was cured. I was a foodaholic. I'm proud I was able to beat that.

Learning that I didn't have to be fat anymore made me realize what I'd been missing from life. For the first time I stopped to smell the roses. I would walk in the park every day, smelling roses. Then I started walking in the park at night, too, because the roses smelled different at night. Then I decided to start *living* in the park, because I couldn't get enough of those roses. I had to smell roses at all hours of the day or night.

Then one night I got mugged in the park and left for dead, and a few hours later, at the hospital, I realized that I had a rose addiction. I went to a special three-times-a-week therapy group for botanical addictions, and it helped a lot, knowing that so many other people could identify with my problem. One of the people in group was Teresa, who had an addiction to the musky scent of zoo animals. Teresa listened to every word I said in group. In fact, Teresa liked me so much that I started going to therapy every night that Teresa was there, whether it was my night or not. From three times a week, I increased my sessions to six, then to seven, and I noticed that people always listened to me when I talked about my various addictions. I started going to therapy sessions in every spare hour I had. Finally I was going to thirty-seven therapy sessions a week, even on the nights when Teresa didn't go.

It was Teresa who first pointed out to me that I was addicted to addiction. And I loved her for that. She suggested that I see a therapist about cutting down on my therapy sessions. So I received counseling for therapy-addiction, and every time I went to a therapy-addiction counseling session, I was able to *eliminate* a botanical-addiction counseling session.

I'm almost finished with the therapy-addiction counseling, now that I'm down to three botanical-addiction sessions a week—and now that I have more free time, I spend it all with Teresa. Three weeks ago I saw her six times in one week. The week after that we went to a resort in Colorado for the weekend. Last week I saw her eighty-seven times. Now that I'm free of all addictions, she's the most important thing in my life. In fact, just thinking of the name Teresa . . . Sorry, gotta take a break here. Be back in a minute.

Okay, great. I'm back. Where were we?

Oh yeah. I was talking about how we'll believe any damn thing anybody tells us about how screwed up we are, and then we'll be *proud* of the fact that we're so screwed up. I've heard so many people bragging about how many drugs they did in the seventies and eighties *but now they don't do em anymore* that I wanna tie em to an iron post and shoot em up with heroin. *Here you go! Stories you can tell in the NEXT century, how about it?*

In fact, I have a new policy about drugs. I'm sick of all the self-righteous bullstuff everybody's spouting, *especially* the people who were drugheads. It goes like this:

Are you reading this book today under the influence of drugs?

Did you just read that sentence and say to yourself, "Hey, how did he know that?"

Do you think it's strange that a book asks you questions and you can't answer back?

Are you in the habit of talking to your book?

Do you ever get up in the morning, look in the mirror, and discover parts of your face missing?

I guess we've all had these experiences at one time or another. Sure, we *say* we're okay. We keep a little heroin around the house, three, maybe four kilos, *just enough* for parties. It's harmless, right? We never shoot in the daytime unless somebody happens to drop by and wants to watch *Leave It to Beaver*. We always know our limit. We never shoot up and drive, cause we don't have a car ever since we sold it to have enough horse for the last party. And we never, ever freebase China White with a blowtorch unless someone else is with us. It's too bad we had to learn this last lesson from Richard Pryor's face gettin burned off.

Is this a description of you? You may not think you have a problem, but you do. You're gettin' ripped off. You're spendin *all your money* on this stuff, so you don't have any left over for dope, booze, punk-rock razorhead parties, or slutty underwear purchases. That's why you need help right now. That's why you need to run, not walk, to the phone and dial 1-800-DRUGGED, where you'll get twenty-four-hour advice from our investment advisers in Bogotá, Colombia. But more than that, you need to change one simple thing about your life. It's easy. It costs you nothing. And it works.

Just say yes.

That's all there is to it. When the beef-face Eyetalian dude in a Giorgio Armani suit shows up at the party flashin horse, just say yes. He's a pusher. And the first one's always free.

When the black dude in purple suede and a cowboy hat moseys out onto your schoolground wavin pills, just say yes. The first one's always free.

When the bleach-blond hooker in a Toni Tennille jungle dress comes up to you in the bar and says, "Hey, good lookin, wanna go up to my room and make a giant fried burrito out of your brain?" just say yes. *Sí. Oui oui.* Eat it, drink it, snort it, watch it do the hula through your blood vessels. Cause you've discovered the secret to kickin the habit: There's *thousands* of these people out there. You can go *years* without repeatin suppliers and keep ever' cent you ever earn. Go ahead, turn your life around today. Your friends might hate you for it, but it's your life they're messin with. They're just tryin to control you.

Let me put it this way. Why do you think they call it a "controlled substance"?

I rest my case.

And while we're on the subject of people who are proud of how screwed up they are, have you noticed how everybody uses this word *dysfunctional* all the time, like:

"You're dysfunctional!"

"I was in a very dysfunctional relationship." (Translation: he was a jerk.)

"I grew up in a dysfunctional family." (Translation: we yelled a lot.)

But the ones that get me are the people who are *proud* of it. They want you to know just how dysfunctional they are. They'll tell you how they were *sooooo* dysfunctional that it shaped their personality forever and so now they'll never be able to have a lasting relationship because blah blah blah and they keep changing the color of their hair because this dysfunctional thing happened and they're insecure now and blah blah blah—and they keep using this word, over and over again, like "I'm dysfunctional, and my *family* was dysfunctional, and I'm attracted to dysfunctional people," and after a while you wanna say "Why don't all you dysfunctionals get up a softball team or something?" As my grandma used to say, "That boy needs a hobby."

Anyhow, listen to me:

When you're fourteen years old, *maybe* you can blame your parents for doing all this dysfunctional stuff that screwed you up.

When you're thirty-four years old, you are what's known in America as a "grown-up."

You can't blame it on *them* anymore! Understand?

They might have screwed up the first fourteen, but the last twenty are *yours*.

This whole "dysfunctional" thing is some kind of psychiatrist deal, isn't it? They invented it to make more money.

Cause we all know how life works, right?

You're born.

You make up a bunch of goals and plans.

You don't do any of em.

A bunch of stuff you didn't think of comes along and makes you into something you didn't wanna be.

You whine about being "dysfunctional."

You eat a lot of Mexican food.

You die.

This isn't anything new. This is the way it's always been.

Get over it, okay?

I don't wanna have to explain this again.

Slaying the Inner Weenie

Okay, we're almost to the sex part, so don't give up on me yet. But first I want you to know that the toughest part of your spiritual journey is just starting. We can't go any farther until you get really aggressive about a) exercising your spear, b) sharpening it, and c) whipping it out.

What do I mean by that?

What I mean by that is that even after you've defeated the Dark Princess, you *still* might be a weenie if you don't consciously make an effort to *hate the weenie living inside you.* This becomes more and more difficult every day, because Madison Avenue wants us to believe that *it's okay to be a weenie.* This started about fifteen years ago, with the famous "Let's all be wimps together" Lowenbrau commercials, and it's carried on today in the form of—you know what I'm gonna say, don't you?—in the form of . . . Cotton Dockers goonies.

How would you like to grab one of those Cotton Dockers guys by each leg of his khaki pants and make a wish?

How would you like to take his foam-soled deck shoe and force it under a Lawn Boy?

What if the next time he stuck his hand in his low-riding diagonal side pocket, there was a two-foot baby rattler in there?

Close-up on his elbow: "Remember those prizes they put in the candy boxes?"

Close-up on the other guy's belt buckle: "Yeah, I always got the little plastic donkeys."

Close-up on the first guy's expanding Adam's apple: "Yeowwwwww!"

Close-up on the Chinese guy's kneecap: "So what snake bit you?"

Close-up on the guy mending the kite: "Whose idea was it to make kites anyway?"

Close-up on the left earlobe of the guy with glasses: "It sure wasn't his—his hand has giant purple snakebites all over it!"

Close-up on the first guy's inseam as he doubles over in pain, grabbing one hand with the other: "AAAAAAARGH! Get me to a hospital! I'm dying!"

Close-up on the back of the first guy's writhing head as he falls down on the wet grass and slides under the greenskeeper's riding lawn mower: "EEEEEEEEEEEEEyooooowwwwwwwwwwwww! Call my family! Get me an ambulance!"

Close-up on the black guy's arms as he chips a nine-iron to the green: "All I need now is a lawn chair and a submarine sandwich, one of those with nine different meats and seven cheeses."

Close-up on the first guy's closely trimmed sideburns, now streaked with blood: "Don't you understand? I'm DYING!"

Close-up on the other four guys leaning against a pier, playing the rock-scissors-paper game: "How can I be cheating? It's impossible to cheat at this game."

Close-up on the first guy's eighty-dollar knit shirt as his four friends grab him by each arm and each leg: "Aren't you supposed to do this with a chicken bone?"

Close-up of the first guy exploding into eight pieces: "If you're not wearing Dockers, you're just wearing pants."

Close-up of the Chinese guy's left ankle: "I wonder who invented chicken bones."

Wouldn't this be nice? But, like I say, the advertising guys have almost convinced us that it's *healthy* to be hanging out with four other weenies as colossally *lame* as you are. You've got to *fight for your right to be male.* This is the nineties. This is war.

You know what I found out recently? We don't even have the right to *sweat* anymore. That's *another* thing Madison Avenue is trying to take away from us, with the triple-extra-strength Arrid double-dry Sahara Desert suck-those-liquid-molecules-out-of-there deodorant commercials.

Do you realize that some chemists in Philadelphia recently figured out the formula for B.O.?

A huge team of scientists successfully isolated "3-methyl-2-hexanoic acid" by sticking giant sponges under the armpits of construction workers that never take showers. Then they took the pads off, stuck em under a microscope, and searched for the B.O. compound. Now they can *bottle* the stuff if they want to.

Now that we've figured this out, though, I want all the wives, girlfriends, and assorted females reading this to listen up:

It's *normal.* It's *natural.* It's a goldurn chemical ingredient that comes out of our body ever' day like God intended. We're *supposed* to smell like that. So lighten up on it, all right?

I called up Wanda Bodine as soon as I saw this in the paper, and I said, "Remember last week when you told me I was disgusting because my armpits smelled like a dead three-ton alligator gar?"

"No, what I said was that your whole *body* smelled like a

dead alligator that had been *carved* into hundreds of pieces and left in the sun for twelve days."

"Well, whatever. My point is that you weren't smelling *me.* You were smelling a chemical that was *on* me. You were smelling a little 3-methyl-2-hexanoic acid."

"Well, whatever I was smelling," she said, "it was Super Unleaded."

"You see, Wanda, you try to make body odor into a *personal* thing. It would be one thing if you were just saying, 'Hey, bozo, you got a little methyl on your skin.' That would be the same thing as saying, 'You got some parmesan cheese in your beard.' It's something you say to a friend. It's *helpful.* But when *you* talk about it, it's like saying, 'You've got something wrong with your *character.'* A little B.O. and you think a person is a degenerate."

"Joe Bob," she said, "it would be different if we were talking about a *little* methyl-hexadragon on your skin."

"Three-methyl-2-hexanoic acid."

"But we're talking about nine thousand pounds of caked armpit concentrate. They could use you for a human chemical weapon."

"But it's *natural,*" I told her. "I thought you *liked* natural things. I thought you were steamed because women are *forced* to shave their legs all the time."

"If I didn't shave my legs," she said, "you'd have some smart-aleck remark to make. That's why I shave my legs."

"I wouldn't have any smart-aleck remark to make. I'd probly say something like 'Hey, Bride of Kong! Nice calves!' But that's what I'm telling you—it's the *same thing.*"

"It is *not* the same thing. I'm forced to shave my legs because of the expectations of other people."

"And I'm forced to spray stuff in my armpits—*endangering*

the environment every time I do it—because of the expectations of *you*."

"B.O.," she said, "is something that infringes on the rights of others."

"No, that's what I'm *telling* you, Wanda. B.O. is *natural.* It's all the *other* smells that infringe on the rights of others, because they're not *natural*."

"Are you saying that everyone should smell like a Shetland pony?"

"No, I'm saying that some people should smell like rhinoceros vomit. It depends on the culture you come from."

"Well, I'll tell you one thing that'll make you take care of your B.O."

I hate it when she gets like this.

"What?"

"If you *don't* take care of it, I'm not shaving my legs, I'm not wearing makeup, and"—here she paused for dramatic effect—"I am *not* shaving my armpits."

"Wanda?"

"Yes."

"I'll have to call you back. I've got to go take a shower."

There are some things too disgusting to imagine, even if they *are* natural.

See, that's how they win. For every disgusting thing a man does, a woman can do something *nine times* as disgusting. But I'm getting ahead of myself. It's time for the real battle now. It's time to meet the enemy.

I'll give you a hint: they wear panty hose.

Preparing Your Inner Warrior to Lie His Ass Off

Now pay real close attention to this part, because this one chapter could save your life someday soon.

The young brave is lost in the woods. He's terrified. He's disoriented. He's hacking away with his sword, left and right, trying to fight his way out. Suddenly, he appears to be saved:

> At the moment of the young brave's greatest despair, a Golden Queen appeared to him in a clearing of the forest. "I know who you are and I have come to save you," she said. The young brave was so stricken with her beauty that he couldn't speak. "You must promise one thing," said the queen. "You must promise to reveal to me your inmost self." Then the young brave knelt before the Golden Queen, bowed his head before her beauty, and said, "Everything I have is yours." And the Golden Queen cut off his head.

You can't fall for the old Golden Queen trick. We have a name for it in modern relationships: "total honesty." What that means is *you* be totally honest, and the *other person* uses your total honesty to rip your guts out.

Every year I try to reform. Every year I tell myself, "Okay, this year, no lies." When this year started, I even made a list of New Year's resolutions, and the first one was "Stop lying to people." But the rest of the list kinda got in the way:

1. Stop lying to people.

2. If you have to lie, limit it to women. They expect it, and they know you're lying even when they say they believe you. So you can treat this *as though you are forgiven* for any lie, because she wouldn't *lie* about believing you, would she?

3. When you lie to a woman, deny that it's a lie until she's in a good mood. Then admit you lied, but deny that you lied about not lying. Tell her you "misunderstood the question."

4. On those rare occasions when you're forced to lie, make sure it's for an important reason, like your whole family will die unless you lie, or your car will be repossessed, or you'll be forced to eat at McDonald's, or you'll be late to the Knicks game (unless you lie).

5. After you tell a real whopper, don't make it worse by denying to *yourself* that your nose just grew eight feet. If you start lying to yourself, then you won't know when you're *telling* a lie, and when you're actually telling *the truth as you know it,* which happens to be pure fiction. This can totally confuse you, so that, when you need to lie, you might screw up and tell the truth instead.

6. If you do start lying to yourself, lie to yourself about *everything* so that you'll be clinically insane, and therefore not

responsible for any of the lies you tell, including the lies you told before you became clinically insane.

7. If you're declared clinically insane, learn to lie to the examining doctor *in a convincing way*. Since the doctor already knows you're a liar, the only way to get out of the asylum is to tell him that you *know* you're a liar, you know you've been lying for a long time, and there is nothing you would like better than to be free of your compulsion to lie. All of these statements are, of course, lies.

8. If you lie to the doctor and *get away with it,* consider a career in clinical psychology.

9. If you get caught lying by a court of law, learn the difference between the lies that hurt you (anytime there's a witness) and lies that help you (anytime there's *no* witness). Admit to hundreds and hundreds of lies that have *absolutely no bearing on your case*. This will help you greatly when you lie about actual felonies.

10. Practice saying "Are you calling me a liar?" Never make the mistake of saying "Do you think I *am* a liar?" Do you see the distinction here?

11. Take that real estate course you've been thinking about.

12. Find out how much it costs to go to law school.

Of course, the real problem is that men don't know how to lie as *effectively* as women. Women know how to tell the absolute truth, but to tell it in such a way that they get more out of it than if they had lied. And then they have the added advantage of being morally superior to us, because we're trying to explain why we lied in the first place.

Some people have become so confused that they don't even

try anymore—they just use *written messages.* Have you seen these Tolstoy novels they're selling as greeting cards now? The ones that take three hours to read, because they're all about how someone "finally found the words to tell you how I feel about you"? The ones that say what a "great person" you are "with so much to offer the world"?

They have watercolor backgrounds, and they always start off with some headline like "Our Love, Endless Love."

Somebody sent me one of these babies the other day—the one that starts out "I'm Concerned About You."

Uh-oh.

Beware of any greeting card that begins with something your sixth-grade teacher would say.

"There's no easy way to say this," it begins.

And I'm thinking, "No easy way to *say* it? Where'd you get the printing press to *print* it?"

"There's no easy way to say this, but I wouldn't be your friend if I didn't let you know. I'm worried about you. You're changing. . . . Our friendship is changing. And I can't just stand by and let that happen. I believe in you. . . . And it hurts me deeply to see you hurting yourself this way."

And then, four hours later, after listing all the ways this person wants me to "find some help," it says: "I care about you . . . I'm concerned about you . . . and now, more than ever, I want to be your friend."

And it has a name after the last line: "Molly Wigand."

I don't know any Molly Wigand.

And then it hit me: Molly Wigand is the *author* of the greeting card. It's her by-line.

Somebody who's concerned about me, but didn't have the guts to tell me, or didn't have the verbal skills to manipulate me with a letter, hired Molly Wigand, a *professional* manipulator.

Do you understand the implications of this? They have hundreds of these cards now. They have one that starts out "I love your sense of humor" and goes on to list 367 things that "I" like about "you" and reasons that we'll always be in love—a great one to send if you're not sure whether the other person is in love or not. They have one called "To My Child" that goes on and on about all the things the parent used to do "when you were hurting or afraid," but now it's time "to let you grow from your mistakes and heartaches"—in other words, don't come whining to *me*. There's one for Dad, about how he never says anything "but you never fooled me—I always knew how much you cared"—perfect for the son who has no idea whether he cared or not.

And then there's one *especially* sly one that starts out "I feel so good about us. It seems not a day goes by that I don't hear about another divorce or breakup, or someone who's miserable but stays in a relationship because 'someone' is better than 'no one.' And when I hear these things, I can't help but be thankful for you. . . ." You get the idea. We *must* be happy, because there are a lot of people more pitiful than we are.

Now we have a whole new reason to buy greeting cards. They're not just something you buy to get past somebody's birthday or anniversary. They're not just something you buy to make yourself feel good about doing all the family obligations that you don't really wanna do but you'll feel guilty if you don't. They're now entire letters you can send to people in order to *lie to them in just the right way*.

This is great! People like Molly Wigand could eventually become best-selling authors, as they discover people who love to manipulate other people in the exact same way that they do.

"Are you Molly Wigand?" they'll say in airports. "I can't believe it! I've been an admirer of yours for so long. I used your 'To a Super Mom' message to get the old bat off my back. But my favorite was 'Remember when we played goofy games together and couldn't stand for the day to end?' That was your best one.

When I gave that to my husband, he almost believed there was a time when we *did* play goofy games together."

My personal favorite is "I never meant to hurt you and I'm really sorry that I did," which goes on for a couple pages and ends in "Please believe me—I never meant to hurt you."

I'm sending in my own composition to Hallmark Cards this week. It goes like this:

"I meant to hurt you. When two people are as close as we are, they get on each other's nerves. My tongue can be a cattle prod, and I know it frightens you and makes you feel alone and separated. This was my intention. I'm tired. I want a divorce. We could save a lot of money on lawyers if you would just see that, after all we've been through together, we have a lot of valuable furniture. I would like some of that furniture. You would like some of that furniture. Let's make it a clean break, because, re-member—I meant to hurt you.

I think my card has a bigger potential market, don't you?

Anyhow, I think you get the idea. I'm going ahead with the dangerous male-female part of the book now. But, just in case you still don't feel confident about it, I'm going to reprint a special mail-order offer that I send out periodically to confused males who want a little extra insurance. I would advise you to send in your money now if you have *any doubts at all* about your ability to enter the dating world and come out alive. Here's the complete offer:

Dear Future Cardholder:

Are we seriously suggesting that you carry *another* credit card?

You bet we are! Because the One-Night Stand VISA card is like *no other*. It works for peace in your life, security in your home, and safety in your night-life environment—every single time you use it.

When you become a cardholder, One-Night Stand contributes $2.00 to the ex-girlfriend and/or ex-boyfriend of your choice. This money will be spent according to your instructions. You might choose option A, the purchase of a greeting card that says "I've never stopped thinking of you." One-Night Stand will be happy to fake your signature from your application form. Or perhaps you'll choose option B, for the kind of ex-lover who would appreciate a direct cash payment. But most people choose option C—a continuing, interest-bearing fund that accumulates capital against that day when you *need it the most*. Diseases, "surprise" pregnancies, assault-and-battery when she finds out, bail bonds . . . we know how nasty love can be in the 1990s, and that's why we've designed One-Night Stand VISA just for you.

Then, *each and every time* you use the card—no matter how small the purchase—we donate another 5¢ to the same cause . . . at no cost to you. Do you see the beauty here? You can be spending money on Bambi at the same time that money is work-ing to keep Carla *off your back*. And since we know how difficult that quick separation can be for some of you working *gals* out there, One-Night Stand also has a twenty-four-hour 800 number for avoiding the hassle and embarrassment of being forced to call the police. Modeled after the AAA emergency towing service, this service can have goons at your door within twenty minutes, fully equipped to throw the geek into the nearest Dempster Dumpster. And it's all paid for by your One-Night Stand VISA.

Just by signing up you'll be helping. In 1989 and 1990 over $150,000 was donated to troublesome ex-partners, many of whom had seen the movie *Fatal Attraction*. Many of those people were potential ax murderers, but once they were appeased by One-Night Stand, 41 percent decided "He really did care about me." Another 29 percent decided "He never has found anybody else and I'm *glad.*" And 89 percent actually wrote letters, similar to this one: "You're so pitiful that I can forgive you now." Only 6 percent committed actual crimes of violence, and in those cases One-Night

Stand stepped in to make certain they were prosecuted and remained behind bars until alternative living arrangements, identities, and jobs could be found for the cardholders.

The One-Night Stand VISA. Send for it today. Don't get lucky without it.

What Men Want, What Women Want, What the Inner Man Wants, What the Inner Woman Wants, and Why the Spear Has a Mind of Its Own

Okay, so far we've been talking basically about Male Stuff. Stuff we understand about each other, even if we don't admit it. Now it's time to do what we always do—screw up a perfectly good thing by introducing nonmales into the equation. This is your guide to what men want in a woman, what women want in a man, and why there's no such thing in either case.

First let's talk about the visual thing. Women don't understand why men will go bird-dogging around after anything in a piece of ten-cent Spandex. To illustrate this, every year I publish something called the annual Joe Bob Briggs Swimsuit Column, proving that the animal imagination of the male *doesn't even need pictures to get totally out of control.*

I'm gonna show you what I mean. Please pay close attention and don't go flippin through it to get to the good parts. This is a fashion service.

In our first paragraph is the lissome Connie, who learned to spell *lissome* this year. The fleshy part of Connie's bronzed bulbous hooters, the part that gets all scrunched up in the middle and casts a shadow in the crack, is held in place by a purple-and-black flower print with neck-string halter, tied underneath a stack of wavy blond hair that slips down over the left edge of her tinted sunglasses. The lips could do urban renewal in Baltimore. She's wearin something else, too, I forget. Weight of swimsuit: 2 ounces. Price: $139.99.

In our second paragraph we have Lila, outfitted in one of those one-piece V-neck babies that crosses over about yay high, lifts, separates, and basically advertises for business. Down at leg level, it sort of scoops up the hip, makes the shape of Florida down the thigh, and gets lost in there somewhere around Key West, cause it's tighter than a convention of rubber bands. Lila has her right hand back behind her ear, her head thrown back, her elbow stuck up in the air, like she's about to shot-put a surfer. Swimsuit weight: 2.6 ounces. Price: $104.95.

Things really get interesting now in our third paragraph, where Jean-Marie is wearing the "Untamed Animal" backless peacock-pattern black-and-tan hyena suit, which looks roughly like somebody cut the stomach out of a leopard, pasted it on the front of her body, and hoped it was legal. Jean-Marie's hair is ruffled up like a rag mop to give her that eat-you-alive look, and her left hip is completely swung across her right leg, even though she's standin up, like she's about to kung fu somethin directly behind her. Husband-hunter's dream. Weight: 3.2 ounces (includin the scrunched-up stuff around the chest). Price: $178.

Now make way for Colleen, who has exactly 3.8 percent of her body covered. On top we got one of those straight-line band dealies, with a twist right over the cleavage that makes it look so deep that Evel Knievel couldn't jump it. Down south, we're talkin strings on the sides, tied in little curlicues that look like if you just *barely* touched em, then . . . Weight: one-eighth of an ounce. Price: $879.95.

Finally, we got Pamela, and I think you know what's comin. We're talkin fishnet. We're talkin big ole holes cut out of the sides and the stomach. We're talking total hip-bone exposure cause the thing crawls up her leg like a horny congressman. And, of course, we're talkin that kinda material that *wiggles* on a dead-still day. It's either blue or red or yellow, I can't remember. It weighs 1.6 ounces. It costs $999, and I'd like to get married to it.

You see what I mean? *I'm* getting out of control, and I *made this stuff up.* Women don't understand this visual thing, where you're sitting in the restaurant with your girlfriend and Christie Brinkley walks by and so *you stare at Christie Brinkley*—and it *doesn't mean diddly-squat.* I mean, we *wish* it meant diddly-squat, but deep down in our hearts, we know it don't mean diddly-squat.

Or should I say that women *used to* not understand this? Because lately I've noticed that, all of a sudden, perfectly normal, ordinary girlfriends—the same girlfriends who *don't want you to stare at Christie Brinkley*—are buying Christie Brinkley swimsuits so that *men they don't know will stare at em!*

Are you following this?

Have you noticed, for example, how *Playboy* has become more respectable than *National Geographic?*

It used to be that every father's nightmare was that his nineteen-year-old cheerleader daughter would come home one day and say, "This wonderful man from *Playboy* wants to take pictures! Of me!" And then Mom would start crying, and Dad would kick the little good-for-nothing bimbo out of the house, and pretty soon she'd be seen in the audience at a Prince concert with Rob Lowe.

But now it's like winning Miss America.

"You got eight nekkid pages in *Playboy?!* Oh my God, I'm *sooooo* happy for you!"

Cause we're talking the big bucks here. We're talking movie deals. We're talking appearances for the next fifteen years at the Santa Monica Car Show. Maybe we're talking Vegas. We're talking swimsuit calendars out the wazoo.

Course, twenty years ago, none of this stuff mattered anyhow. But now, if you've got a career, you've *got a life.*

A couple years back I wrote an article for *Playboy* on the "Queens of the B's"—actresses like Monique Gabrielle and Linnea Quigley who have become superstars in horror flicks—and when the article came out, it was accompanied by photos of about ten of em *in flagrante torpedo,* with the headline "B-Movie Bimbos!" I called up my editor and said, "How can you do this to me? These women will *kill* me! You called em all *bimbos! All* of em!"

And he said, "Oh, don't worry about it. We told em the title of the article in advance. Their managers knew it. They knew it. They said it was fine."

Talk about publications with power.

You used to pose for *Playboy* at the *beginning* of your career, when you were *not* respectable. Now you do it when you're a star, to *prove* you're respectable.

And then the *next* stage is, "I don't do nudity anymore."

After you do the most public nudity there is.

I'm still working on this. I'm still trying to figure it out.

They *wanna* be called bimbos, and they *don't* wanna be called bimbos. They *want* me to see em nekkid, and they *don't* want me to see em nekkid.

So which is it? Please write in and help me out on this.

Meanwhile, there's one thing I'm dead certain about, and it's that even though more and more women want to take off all their clothes for men, there are *also* more and more women who *don't want men looking at nekkid women.* (The only reason I'm making such a big deal out of this is so you can see how dangerous it is even to *bring up the subject.*)

For example, there's this judge in Florida who says you can't hang up pictures of the "Miss February *Iron Horse* Biker Bikini Girl" over your desk anymore. They were tackin em up on lockers at the Jacksonville shipyards, and a welder named Lois Robinson got her feelings hurt because nobody had ever asked *her* to be the "Miller Lite Hooter Honey" for the Greater St. Petersburg area, so she decided her workplace was full of "sexual harassment."

And she *won the case!* The feminists helped her file her lawsuit, and she *won!* All the nekkid women have to be ripped down off the wall.

They got their wish.

They've finally made it an *actual crime* to think about sex with a strange woman, or to even *talk* about it in the presence of a woman, or even to be *thinking* about it.

Is America ready for this?

I don't think the judge went far enough. I think there are a whole *bunch* of things on the wall we need to have laws against.

For example, I think anybody that has the oil painting of the "Poker-Playing Dogs" on his wall ought to go straight to state prison. I don't wanna be forced to *look* at that. It offends me. It constitutes harassment of my life.

Or what about those giant steel modern-art girders lying on the sidewalk in front of the Citicorp Crown Centre Bankplace Towers? You know, the ones that look like somebody bent a wire coat hanger into the shape of a Gumby doll that's been ripped apart with a pair of pliers.

I'm *appalled* by this display. It affects my ability to do my job.

In fact, let's talk about these people that put stickers on their car that say "Divers Go Deeper" and "I Love My Tibetan Wolfhound" and "This Lifetime Brought to You by Jesus." Are these people obnoxious or *what?* Maybe we could find a federal judge who would say it's illegal to invade my space with anything that makes me *cringe.*

Bad shirts! Maybe we could get rid of em once and for all. Especially the ones the winos down on Akard Street wear. The ones that look like Leroy Neiman threw up on them.

Even more important, anybody whose underwear sticks up out of the top of their pants. Some guys have jockey shorts riding up so high that their faces are puckered.

In other words, maybe this judge has done us a favor. If you can force us to rip down pictures of women who are, let's face it, better looking than 99 percent of the population, then just *think* what we'll be able to get rid of. We may never have to look at the Ford Taurus again.

Kinda got off the subject there, but you can see what kind of confusing sexual signals men are getting these days. Then, on top of all that, this article comes out in *Psychology This Week* saying that men's brains have gotten scrambled in the nineties, and they don't even *like* the most beautiful women anymore.

The article says that men don't want "tens" anymore. They want women to be "nines." They interviewed all these guys who talked about how the Bo Derek standard was out. I didn't quite understand what they were saying, since I thought a "ten" was whatever you personally thought was bodacious, but I think the reasoning goes like this:

"Tens" are too perfect. They look like mannequins in a department store. If you want a man's insides to go all gooey, show him a woman with a crooked nose, or fingers that are too long for the rest of her body, or something like that—and they'll go, "Wow! She's *almost* beautiful!"

It's like a medium-rare steak. "This is *great!* It's *almost* cooked!"

But I don't think the article went far enough. If a Nine is better than a Ten, why isn't an Eight better than a Nine? Think of the advantages for the nineties woman:

Ten: Obviously out. That's why nobody went to Bo Derek's last movie.

Nine: Sexier than a Ten, because she has a little flaw, like thin eyebrows.

Eight: Sexier than a Nine, because she's actually cross-eyed and pigeon-toed, making it obvious that she could never be a Ten, and therefore making her an attainable Dream Woman.

Seven: Better than an Eight, because she has a knife scar on her left cheek for that "Let's party" look.

Six: Better than a Seven, because she's good-looking, but she has body tattoos all over her back, some of them in the shape of extinct reptiles. When she has her clothes on, nobody knows how hideous she is. When she has her clothes off, *who cares?*

Five: One leg shorter than the other, bunions, and a hiney the size of Saudi Arabia. This woman could walk down Fifth Avenue buck nekkid in the daytime and the Turkish cab drivers wouldn't even notice her. She can be yours forever.

Four: Now we're getting into the real Dream Woman. A Four has buck teeth, a bowl haircut, and a body like the Tasmanian devil. Moss grows on her teeth. Dogs take four-block detours to avoid her. This woman will not only notice you, she'll be *grateful* to you.

Three: This woman has two extra fingers on her left hand, a mustache, and weighs 230 pounds. She knows how to belch the themes of popular show tunes.

Two: Men in the nineties will be drooling over this goddess, who was born with six arms and a tail. She can make your dinner, give you a massage, and clean the wax out of her ears all at the same time. And to think, in the eighties, she would have been considered freaky.

One: Finally, the woman all sensitive nineties men are dreaming about. Her name is Tammy Faye Bakker.

I *want* that woman.

Actually, though, I don't totally buy this article, because at the same time it came out, there was a syndicated TV show called *Dream Girl USA* that I became totally fascinated with. (I'm getting to the point here in a minute. Bear with me.) And this show, *Dream Girl USA,* comes on Channel 21 Sunday morning right after rodeo and right before Jimmy Swaggart, and the basic idea is you take all your rejects from the Miss Providence, Rhode Island, beauty pageant and you ask em to come out to Hollywood and stay at the Hilton three days and sing "Oklahoma" with their hands on their hips and wear stiletto high heels and aerobics clothes and answer the weekly "think on your feet" question, which is always something like "What is your favorite Bee Gee and why?" Then, all the time they're doing this, there's a panel of celebrity judges, guys like Ziggy "the Animal" Liebowitz, head of Liebowitz and Frick Productions, who produced *Celebrity Safari* for Canadian syndication, and Wilhelmina Swanson, head of the Swanson Agency, which did all the casting for *Rat Patrol: The Second Edition.* And the celebrity judges are hitting these automatic electronic gong buttons that flash points up on the screen, so as soon as Desiree Dillard from East Winnebago,

Kansas, stops pounding out the "Christian Hits of Amy Grant" medley on a baby grand piano while grinnin like a Siamese jackal, they can zap a big ole "27" up on the screen, to show that she didn't do diddly, and then whoever's left over at the end gets to come back for the semifinals and try to win some more nail polish.

It's great.

I watch it ever' week.

Here's the best part of the deal: the "up close and personal" interviews with the contestants. Like here's one with Faith Jernigan of Stillwater, Oklahoma, who's a day-care assistant at Interstate 40 Babtist Church when she's not having her body waxed in preparation for *Dream Girl USA:*

"When I really feel like splurging, I have my boyfriend take me to Baskin-Robbins. On most days of the week I eat yogurt. You have to when you're trying to watch that figure. But then I'll say to myself, 'Faith, you *deserve* some of the banana-nut surprise,' and I just feel so *guilty.* But that's what I like about life here in Stillwater. It's the kind of place where you can take it easy, be with your friends, be whoever I want to be, and someday I hope to be able to use my personal skills as a people person to settle down and do something wonderful with my life in the advertising and public relations field. That's why *Dream Girl USA* is so important to me. This is a great country, and God loves you."

I'm telling you, *watch this show.* You don't believe me. I *know* you don't believe me. You *cannot* get this on the network.

So, as you can see, feminism only goes *so far* in America. Keep this in mind when you're trolling for a date.

And then there's the other side of the meat-market coin. One thing most men forget when they're looking for nookie is that *most women are just as desperate as you are.* Believe me, you do not wanna realize this ten years from now in a divorce court somewhere in West Virginia.

Go to any bookstore and look at the racks in the women's

section. Believe me, all the bimbos of America go to B. Dalton's twice a year and buy a paperback about how to manipulate us into marrying em and then spending the rest of our lives shopping at Hancock's Fabric Outlet with em and *not* whining about it. The perfect man for the nineties is evidently some guy that knows how to lay bathroom tile, works at J. C. Penney's, and thinks Valerie Harper is the perfect woman.

Here's some of the sick stuff on the shelves:

Rich Men, Single Women, by Adriana Gabrielle: Tells you how to shop for hipless string bikinis in West Palm Beach.

Women Who Lunch Too Much, by Vivian Poole: This woman researched the mating habits of desperate Beverly Hills cheesecake and found that many of them didn't find the ideal man because they were too busy ordering spinach tortellini on Rodeo Drive.

Men Who Hate Women's Guts and Deserve to Die, by the Berkeley Women's Consortium: Describes the Dirty Harry Syndrome among married women over forty. Extensive firearm photo section.

Baby-Talk for Success, by Jennifer Monique Paley: This millionaire Houston businesswoman managed to capitalize a $10 million import-export business in three days without using a dime of her own money. How'd she do it? "Sweetums doesn't *know* how she do it," she reveals in Chapter 12.

Shop Smart, Date Smart, Marry Smart, by Maria Angelina Parilla, a penniless Cuban immigrant in 1982 who used nothing more than her thirty-eight-inch hooters and several yards of clingy silk to become one of the most powerful women in Sioux City, Iowa.

Divorce Smart, by Maria Angelina Parilla: Her sequel, in which she reveals the investment strategies that brought her $30 million in two years.

If I'm So Wonderful, Why Do Men Look at Me Like I'm a Crippled Warthog? by Constance Bogard: Deals with the common problem of women who were born with a condition known as "ugly."

Anorexic and Proud! by Fran Frawley: Explodes the myth of nutrition. Released shortly before her untimely death.

Daddy's Little Sweet-Potato Baby, by Eleanor Stephenson: Contains a directory of over 5,000 American men who *prefer* fat girls, with descriptions of the ones who have the financial means to maintain a full twenty-four-hour feedlot with salad bar within their homes.

Bag One Before the Hips Go, by Susie Carpenter: The bible for seventeen-year-olds who can't get into college.

So don't say I didn't warn you.

Actually, one of the best ways to meet that special woman who will *believe anything* is to buy a personal ad. But even *that* has changed in the nineties.

I hadn't been gettin any action on my personal ad, "Musky Writer Sniffing for Nookie," so I decided to look around for new copy. "Musky" has been running pretty much nonstop since 1984, and even though I've found several women I was willing to spend up to three days with, it's obvious I'm gonna need something new for the nineties.

But if you haven't looked at the personals lately, you might be pretty shocked to see exactly what the new American woman *does* want in the nineties. Or, rather, what she does *not* want. Really she doesn't want anything. She just wants to make sure you're not one of *those*.

A typical "Woman Seeks Man" ad goes like this:

"Slender 5' 7" redhead, age unimportant, weight proportional to height . . . "

Of course, we all know what this means. She's a grandma the size of the Seattle Kingdome.

" . . . seeks relationship with straight man. No fatties. No druggies. No diseases. No jocks. No smokers. No hard-rock types. No heavy drinkers. Must own your own home. No God's-gift-to-women types. No cowboys. No playboys. No dishonesty. No religious freaks. No little boys trying to be men. No rednecks. Must love cats. Must be financially secure. No workaholics. No boring, overeducated types. No schizophrenics. Not interested in someone who expects 'the little woman' to cook and clean for him. No one-night stand artists. No demands. Let's talk."

Can you imagine the guy who shows up to *answer* one of these ads? What's he gonna say? "I've been looking for a woman like you all my life"? Actually, he'd better say "Excuse me." The nineties are gonna be the decade when the woman starts nagging you *before you even meet her.*

Now, for reasons I'll go into later on, it's been my theory for a long time that the only goal of most women today is to hook up with some guy for about, oh, six months, just long enough to be sure they can get safely pregnant. The first five months are the "safety" part. Once the guy passes his physical, they get that biological clock primed and buy some digital chromosome meter in the drugstore or something, and they know *exactly* when they need to have sex in order to pop out a little yard monster nine months later, long after the guy has been chunked into the Dempster Dumpster. They figure, "Hey, he's leaving anyway, right? Might as well get some use out of him."

So, anyhow, this knowledge, combined with my close study of the "Woman Seeks Man" personals, has resulted in my new Joe Bob Briggs can't-miss personal ad, which should last well into the late nineties. It goes something like this:

"World famous writer does absolutely nothing with his time and money, needs woman to organize his life and spend his money. Also knows there is some way men can make babies, but requires a loving teacher. Loves to turn off Sunday afternoon football game and go to the botanical gardens with that special someone. Will obtain plastic surgery if necessary. Let's spend a lifetime together, or as much as you're willing to give me."

Believe me, they'll be slobbering all over the page on this one. I'm gonna have nine dates a week.

You kinda get the message here?

They don't know what they want, so *you have to tell em.*

Still wanna go forward? Because, sooner or later, if you keep trying, you're gonna get an actual *date.* Which is a whole new can of worms, because now, whether you like it or not, you've got to actually *do things with em.* For the gritty details, read on.

Joe Bob's Guide to Dating in the Nineties

O kay, you've met the woman. You're in love, or something similar. Now what do you do with her?

First you buy condoms. (We cover *everything* in this book.)

I recently tried to get hired as a professional condom tester, but they said I was "underqualified."

I have no idea what they meant.

Anyhow, before we go any further, it's time for the Joe Bob Briggs Safe-Sex Let's-Beat-This-AIDS-Deal Scientific Birth-Control Survey, and I think you're gonna be a little bit surprised at some of the results. This year we tested ninety-four different brands of condoms, including the new Triple-Ply Corn Husker "Mr. Magic," which is the only condom assembled by hand at a factory in Athens, Georgia. After interviewing Selma Dulles, the sole employee, we wouldn't recommend the Husker for general use.

The highlights of this year's survey:

The Yamabuki No. 2 Lubricated: This is the first year we've tested Japanese condoms, and we finally decided that, hey, there's gotta be *something* in our lives these people don't make money off of. We refuse to recommend these things on principle.

The Ramses Extra with Spermicidal Lubricant and Reservoir End: This used to be a favorite with people who purchase condoms in the rest rooms of country-western bars in the Deep South, but we weren't pleased. We attached the Extra to a helium gas tank, blew it up into a balloon of about eighteen inches in diameter, then twisted it into the shape of an iguana with big ears. At this point the left ear sprung a leak, and we were unable to use the condom. We also had to send the person wearing it to the emergency room, where he is resting comfortably.

The LifeStyles Stimula Vibra-Ribbed: We pumped three and a half gallons of Old Milwaukee into this condom, until it looked like an overinflated beach ball, and then dropped it off a seven-story building onto a bed of nails. The Stimula never ruptured, but the so-called "vibra-ribs" *ceased to vibrate.* We find this unacceptable, especially since we didn't notice the defect until someone had already *used* the same condom later that night. He was very upset.

The Sheik Fetherlite Snug-Fit: To test just how "snug" it was, we pulled this condom down over Luke Springer's head, to see if we could make out his facial features while he was wearing it. Not only could we see the perfect outline of his nose, cheekbones, lips, and chin, but Luke also couldn't breathe, proving that the advertising claims of a total latex "vacuum" during condom use were true! We strongly recommend this brand. (We also ask that if you purchase a Fetherlite, you make a donation to the Luke Springer Memorial Fund.)

The Protex Contracept Plus: *Stinky!* I'm sorry, we don't go any further when we can't get past the opening of the package.

Trojan Kling-Tite Naturalamb: Condoms made out of lamb intestines have always struck us as a little kinky, but we will do *anything* to support the depressed Texas sheep industry. We tried all the usual tests on this one and couldn't break it, so we stuffed it with cherry bombs, threw it in an incinerator, came back four hours later—and it was still in one piece, ready for action. They didn't carry em in Vietnam for nothing.

Finally, we've got your "Lady" brands—Lady Trojan, Lady Protex Ultra-Thin, Lady Excita Extra, Lady LifeStyles Nuda—and, when these first came out, we were skeptical. Can you really trust a woman to buy the condom, use the condom, take care of the condom? Then somebody told us that *the man still has to wear these condoms!* Can you believe this? We've got to do everything already. I don't see the point. What if you die during sex? You want your family to read a coroner's report that says, "Deceased had lacerations on his clavicle, a slight deformity of the left kneecap, and was wearing a Lubricated Lady Fiesta Nude Plus with Ribbing"? I think not.

We'll pass.

Okay, now that that's out of the way, we can continue on with the date proper. First of all, you've got to assume that the woman of your dreams *never ever wants to go anywhere you want to go.* This is just a fact of modern life. So you've got to *assume that the date will be painful.* But that's not important on a first date anyhow. The only thing that matters on a first date is how successfully you can convince this woman that you're not the pathetic loser you know in your heart you are. How can you do that? The best way, I've found, is to suffer through something cultural.

Ladies *love* anything cultural. But do you have what it takes? How cultured are you?

Use the easy and foolproof Joe Bob Briggs Culture Test to find out.

This is so easy, there's only *one question* to answer.

The question is, "Can you sit through an entire performance of . . ."

1. A Frank Sinatra Seventy-fifth Anniversary Tour show, *including* the Regis Philbin warm-up act. If this is as far as you can go, you are *somewhat* cultured. But can you sit through . . .

2. A two-hour PBS special on bluegrass bands from West Virginia, including the part where they talk about their relatives and Robert Klein comes out and explains "the historical significance of native American music." If so, you are *moderately* cultured. But can you sit through . . .

3. The road company of *Les Misérables,* performing at the San Jose Civic Center. Now you're getting into some *serious* cultural obstacles. Most people can't handle this one, but those who can are *extremely* cultured. But there are many more levels to pass through. For example:

4. Guys named Yudi or Yuri or Fiesole who play the violin at Carnegie Hall. They're only a *little* easier to listen to than . . .

5. Guys named Viktor and Brechtov and Vlasic Mycek who play the cello at Lincoln Center. But a *real* cultural test is . . .

6. Anything at the Kennedy Center. People in Washington never wanna be there, never wanna see anything, sleep through everything, so the Kennedy Center is this dumping ground for every Yugoslavian acrobatic troupe on horseback that has ever landed a P.T. boat in Chesapeake Bay. If you can sit through one of these multiethnic borefests, you get a cultural gold card. But now, for those who wanna go platinum, we have . . .

7. Off-off Broadway theaters, the kind of acting groups that have thirty seats in a SoHo loft and think Bertolt Brecht is

really neat. Now you're into areas where people actually scream stuff in your face. You're entering the cultural elite. Next stage:

8. Lesbian ballet. You know what I mean. The kind where they grab one another around the clavicle and form human Slinkys while chanting "The goddess is pure! Death to the musky snake people! Hoist me up by the thighs! The goddess is pure!" At these performances, you can actually *prove* how cultural you are, because sitting through the whole thing causes actual physical pain. Next:

9. Anything called "performance art." Latest variation: anything with kettle drums.

But finally, I think we all know what it takes to be really and truly cultural in America. Do you have what it takes? Can you sit through it? Can you hack it?

I'm speaking, of course, of Garrison Keillor. The man is on the lecture circuit again.

If he dies before he gets to Texas, *I didn't do it.* Really. I would never do that. Really.

And actually, now that I'm thinking about it, there are few more impressive feats, from a woman's point of view, than a male who is able to sit through an entire Neil Diamond concert.

There was this bet I lost back in 1976, when I was trying to get ownership of this trained attack pig that Wanda Bodine bought off of Jimbo Carruthers after his divorce from Randi Lynnette Carruthers whereby they had to sell off all their farm animals to take care of their sleazeball lawyer Warren Randolph Scroggins. Jimbo ended up with all outstanding beauty-care debts, including a fifty-dollar body-waxing job Wanda performed on Randi Lynnette when she was training for the Johnson County Rodeo in barrel racing. Jimbo couldn't come up with the cash, so Wanda ended up with a 350-pound attack pig named Pollywog that would ram his snout through anything you pointed at with a bamboo stick, including ex-wives, and so I had to have him, and so that year Wanda and me made this bet on the Super Bowl that, if I won, I would get total eternal possession of Pollywog the trained attack pig. But if she won—which she did—the stakes were even higher:

I agreed to take Wanda Bodine to the Neil Diamond concert every time he came to Texas for the rest of his or her natural life, whichever one ended first.

In case you haven't heard, he hasn't died yet. In fact, he rolled into Fort Worth a couple of weeks ago wearin a white parachute shirt with Liberace sleeves and foo-foo shoulder pads, cracklin his Rosie all over the state while about 17,000 Lipstick Lizards tanned their rooster necks from the glare off his trick britches. In case you haven't ever seen this, those pants have got more sheen on em than the haircut on a Pentecostal preacher. When he finally gets to "Sweet Caroline," which is the part where I have to recite the Gettysburg Address in my head so I won't throw up on the Toni home permanent in the row in front of me, Wanda Bodine just about rips off her Playtex underwire support bra, runs it up a flagpole, and sends Neil some semaphore signals that say "Please let me into your hotel room so I can dance upside down on your clavichord."

But, believe it or not, that's not the worst part. It's not even when he does "I Am I Said," one of the most profound songs in Western civilization, thanks to the message of that song, which is "He said he is." And it's not when he does "America." Or even "Song Sung Blue," which he was singing the same way in 1976 and every year since then. I know what you're thinking, though. You're thinking that it's gotta be the moment when he does "I'm a Believer" and his gold neck chains reflect from the laser light show directly off the giant bald spot on top of his head.

Nope. That's a definite highlight, but it's nothing compared to . . .

"Forever in Blue Jeans."

Now that most of you have already run screaming out of the room, I'll reveal to the ones that are left that he shouts all the lyrics out in a voice that sounds like a professional sumo wrestler stomping on the larynx of Robin Leach while Leach begs for more interviews with Elizabeth Taylor. Fortunately, this is always the place where Wanda Bodine passes plumb out.

"Beautiful noise, Neil baby," I tell him as I hoist her hiney into the bed of the pick-up. The man's a genius.

Sorry I got off on that. That was disgusting.

You know, I used to think that the perfect place to take a girl on a date was a miniature golf course. It's *almost* sports, so guys like it, and it's got colored balls and cute little windmills, so gals like it. But since then I've had so many *horrifying* experiences at mini-golf courses that I've revised my opinion.

You probly already heard about the worst one.

It's true that they barred me from the Putt-Putt miniature golf course on Coit Road for putting a two-foot dent in a baby elephant, but it wasn't my fault. Mavis Hunley kept knocking her ball into the decorative concrete jungle-swamp water garden because "I like to take a good solid swat at it." And I *told* her not to do that. I told her, "Mavis, they got three-year-old kids that can hit the ball hard enough to get it up to the hole." But Mavis said the game is a good way to take out your aggressions, and so she pretty much smashed the yellow Day-Glo paint off the ball every single time she hit it.

Every time we play miniature golf, I think it's gonna be different. I think we're gonna concentrate on the game, try to *learn* something out there on the course, but then Mavis or Wanda Bodine or Rhett Beavers or *somebody* decides their personal honor is at stake.

Like, if you take Wanda to the golf course, she gets more and more hacked off every time you have to pass one of those seventeen-year-old girls in the blue-jean miniskirts. You know the ones I'm talking about? The ones that are always playing miniature golf with guys named Shane that wear football jerseys that are cut in half across their chest?

These gals, as we all know, don't know how to play miniature golf. We all realize this. We all realize they're gonna put their ball down on the mat and sweep it like their putter's a broom and then giggle. And then, when it goes too far and bounces off the back and comes all the way back down to where it started, they're gonna giggle some more and jump up and down and *hit it again before it stops rolling.* I know this. You know this. Girls in blue-jean miniskirts have been doing this for years. Everybody who has played miniature golf knows this.

Wanda doesn't know this.

"What does she think she's doing?" Wanda will say.

I'll try to explain. "She's jumping up and down so Shane will see her miniskirt."

"See her miniskirt? *See* it? I think we've all seen *enough* of it."

"It's your turn."

"What?"

"It's your turn to play, Wanda. Hit the goldurn ball."

And then, of course, Wanda will hit the ball off the back board and it'll come all the way back down to where it started.

Or you take Mavis. Mavis's problem is kids with purple hair or a lot of chains on their shirt. You know this group, don't you? The group of six, and *none* of them *ever* gets their ball in the hole. Never, ever, not once. They just hit it and then hit it again and then hit it some more, and then they pick it up and start hitting it on the next hole. And when they're not hitting it, they act like they're about to hit one another over the head with their clubs. And when they're not doing that, they all hit their balls at the same time. And when they're not doing that, they *kick* the balls.

"It's punk golf, Mavis. Don't worry about it."

But she can't stand it.

"I'm gonna speak to the manager."

"What good is that gonna do? They can play punk golf if they want to."

"It says here, right on the scorecard, that only one person plays at a time."

"Yeah, right, Mavis. Maybe we'll need the police."

"Five-stroke maximum! Five-stroke maximum!"

"Mavis, they hit the goldurn balls so fast nobody can tell how many times they hit em anyway."

"I saw one guy hit his ball *nine* times on one hole."

"It's your turn."

"What?"

"It's your turn to play."

And that's when Mavis decides she has to take a good solid whack at the ball. And so a few months back, at the time in question, she took a full backswing, like she was in the U.S. Open or something, and she hit the ball so hard that it flew right off the end of the club, bounced off a replica of the Matterhorn, skimmed across a zebra's back, and fell into two feet of water underneath a spraying-trunk baby elephant. I didn't wanna say anything at the time, but it also missed a kid with orange hair by about nine inches.

Fortunately, the kid thought it was really cool.

I didn't want this situation to escalate, though, and so I plunged into the swamp and, in one graceful athletic movement, vaulted over the baby elephant's back and kicked Mavis's ball off the bottom with the side of my boot.

Unfortunately, it landed on the assistant night manager's Adam's apple.

Well, it didn't really land there. It kind of hit there and sprung backward, and when the ambulance came it was . . .

Well, all I've got to say is we could have made $10,000 on *America's Funniest Home Videos* if we'd just remembered to bring the camera.

I think it's a little strict, though, to get barred just for one lousy dent in a baby elephant. I could have reached down in there and beat it back into shape. I used to work for Deke's Auto Body Repair.

"Joe Bob, you've got to learn to stay out of other people's business," Mavis said. "That wasn't your ball."

"That's right," Wanda added. "Serves you right for meddling."

So I think you can see why I no longer recommend miniature golf, at least not on the first date.

And while we're on this subject, speaking of Wanda and Mavis, I might as well get this over with right now. It's another thing you're gonna have to deal with. Women like to talk a *lot* more than men do, so don't be surprised if you're plumb tuckered out halfway through the date.

As a matter of fact, you may have heard that they've been doing Blabbermouth Research at major American universities. They're spending jillions of dollars to find out why people are blabbermouths.

I have a personal interest in this research because one of my friends, Leticia Carruthers, unmarried sister of Jimbo Carruthers, is a professional blabbermouth, the kind of person that when somebody says "It's Leticia on the phone, Joe Bob!" I say something like, "I'll have to call her back. I'm busy walking from the bedroom to the living room right now."

One time I said to Leticia Carruthers, "I'm feeling kinda puny today. My cousin in Kentucky had a head-on collision with a coal truck, and he's been in intensive care for twelve hours. They said his car was mashed flat, and it's a miracle he's alive."

And Leticia said, "I have a car, too. It's this peppy little Mazda that gets twenty-eight miles to the gallon, which I need now that I have to drive into town from Mineral Wells every day, and I was parked at the Burger King when this really cute guy asked me to roll down my window and . . . "

You get the idea here?

You say to Leticia, "I really need to talk."

And Leticia says, "Good, let me tell you about my hysterectomy."

And now they say, after years of research, that Leticia can't help it. She's spewing out all this jabber because she *has* to. She doesn't know what you're saying to her. She doesn't know what she's saying to *you*. She just plain doesn't know what she's saying.

When I found this out, I called her up. "Leticia," I said, "there's something you ought to know."

"Oh, good, did you know that I was thinking about you this morning, Joe Bob, and wondering if you would be calling, because I wanted to tell you about the trip I'm taking next spring to—"

"Shutup, Leticia."

"What?"

"Shutup. This is the first thing I wanted to talk to you about. The meaning of the word 'shutup.' "

Leticia didn't say anything. This is the first time in history, that I can remember, when Leticia had nothing to say.

Rule number one in Blabbermouth Therapy: The blabbermouth is afraid of you. That's why they talk all the time—so that you can't say anything that'll make em feel insecure. That's why "shutup" works. It makes em feel *so* insecure they're ready to commit suicide.

"You don't need to commit suicide about it," I told Leticia. "You just need to listen to me. You are an addict."

"You know," she said, "that's just what my grandma used to

say when she was talking about Grandpa—she'd use that word 'addict.' Of course, she wasn't talking about the same thing, I don't think so anyway, but don't you think it's funny that she used . . . "

"Shutup, Leticia."

Rule number two in Blabbermouth Therapy: After you use "shutup" the first time, the blabbermouth will use any excuse to make believe you never said "shutup" and that nothing has changed. So you have to say it again.

"Leticia," I said. "Listen."

She listened.

"You can hang up on me anytime you want to."

"Oh nooo, Joe Bob, I would never hang up on you."

Rule number three in Blabbermouth Therapy: The blabbermouth can't stand rejection, so he or she will never get mad and leave. The blabbermouth is a blabbermouth *because* he or she can't leave. The blabbermouth needs you more than you need the blabbermouth.

"Leticia, there are times when silence is a good thing."

"I *love* silence, Joe Bob, you are *soooo* right."

Rule number four in Blabbermouth Therapy: The blabbermouth is a liar. The blabbermouth needs to agree with you and needs to know that you agree with the blabbermouth. If you say, "You know, Hitler wasn't such a bad guy after all," the blabbermouth will instantly say, "I've *always* thought that about Hitler, and Goering and Goebbels, too. I liked that Ayatollah guy. He just had a bad publicist."

"Leticia, anything I say, you're gonna agree with it, aren't you?"

"Well, not anything. Well, okay, sure, Joe Bob, I guess I could agree with anything."

Blabbermouths don't like this question.

"And, Leticia, anything I say to you about myself is going to be boring to you, isn't it?"

"Oh nooooo, Joe Bob, I'd love to hear something about yourself. One of my favorite topics is yourself. You're so much like me."

"I'm not like you."

"I didn't mean that you were *really* like me, but you remind me of me."

Rule number five in Blabbermouth Therapy: The more you contradict the blabbermouth, the more the blabbermouth will try desperately to agree with you.

"Let's give it a try, Leticia," I told her. "I'm gonna tell you something about me that has nothing to do with you. Do you understand the concept here?"

"That sounds *very* exciting, Joe Bob."

"And when I start talking about me, we will discuss me. We will not discuss you. We will discuss me. Do you understand this?"

"We will discuss you."

"All right. Here's the topic. I have a bass boat."

"My *uncle* has a bass boat!"

Rule number six in Blabbermouth Therapy: No matter how many times you think you have the blabbermouth under control, you don't. You're deluding yourself. They're addicts. They're incurable. Their uncles always have bass boats.

"Leticia?"

"Yes, Joe Bob."

Rule number seven in Blabbermouth Therapy: You can always get the blabbermouth's attention by saying the blabbermouth's name.

"Leticia, tell me about your uncle's bass boat."

Rule number eight in Blabbermouth Therapy: You can always leave the phone off the hook. Go about your business. Every five minutes return to the phone and say one of the two following phrases:

"Uh-huh."

Or,

"No, I hadn't heard that."

Rule number nine in Blabbermouth Therapy: Never ask a question. This extends any blabbermouth conversation a full hour.

Rule number ten in Blabbermouth Therapy: Never, ever, under any circumstances, ask about a hysterectomy.

Okay, Joe Bob, that's enough on that subject. Shutup.

Before I forget, there's one other thing you should never, ever, under any circumstances, talk to a woman about: her weight.

Wanda Bodine came in the other day and said she had joined the Grapevine chapter of Overeaters Anonymous. I was very understanding.

"You mean Lard Unlimited? The circus tents with feet that meet in the back room of the Burger King?"

Wrong thing to say.

"There's a reason we meet there," Wanda told me. "It's part of our acceptance of our illness."

"I can see that. It's *really* the home of the Whopper now."

After I got back from the Emergency Room, Wanda and I continued our discussion. Wanda explained that she had learned in college to eat the four major food groups at every meal. The problem was, she thought you were supposed to eat *every* food in every food group at every meal.

"They need to make that more clear in the textbooks," she said.

Then, when she got to be around twenty-three, twenty-four, she started eating to relieve tension. This meant some serious poundage on the nights she had to drive in the Demolition Derby. Sometimes she'd finish off forty, fifty Super Dogs *while* she was driving, and then after that she'd grab a handful of those little plastic relish dealies and suck out all the green stuff.

"I was a mess," she said. "I was beginning to lose all self-respect. I would look in the mirror and deny that I was really me."

"I've done that before."

"You have?" said Wanda.

"Yeah. Course, it doesn't matter if I deny I'm me, because I'm not fat like you."

"Then I started eating alone—after work, before work, during work. I *lived* to eat. I would decide to stop eating, but that would make me so nervous I would have to eat. So I would decide to stop deciding to stop eating, and I would eat. That worked for a while, because when I ate, instead of stopping eating, I didn't have the desire to eat. But then after that I'd want to eat again."

"Meanwhile," I said, "you're porking up like a Holstein."

"The only thing that could stop me was myself, but I was denying that myself was myself. There were occasional little signs that I was out of control, like the night I ate three hundred and forty-seven bags of cheese-flavored Doritos after dinner."

"That was you? I thought somebody invited over a herd of Australian wild boars to watch a little TV."

"Not only that," said Wanda, "I had to start buying my clothes from the National Aeronautics and Space Administration."

"You always did look good in silver."

"And then, of course, you know what finally brought me to the end of it? It was last spring when the Texas Parks and Wildlife Department started talking about the new law to create a season for Wanda Bodine hunting."

"Did that really bother you that much?"

"I was humiliated."

"I think they were only kidding. It was just gonna be two days. You could of holed up in the trailer house."

"I was already receiving cash offers to visit game preserves."

"You're making much too big a deal out of it. They only allowed small-caliber rifles and crossbows."

"I finally saw myself for what I was. I knew I had to get help. That's when I started attending Lard Unlimited."

"That's a touching story, Wanda. I hope that some day you won't look like a twelve-ton farm animal."

"Thank you, Joe Bob."

"Just the fat-folds alone are gonna be disgusting, though."

"I know I can do it—one day at a time."

"I love you like a balloon in the Macy's Thanksgiving parade in the shape of a giant flesh-eating walrus."

"I love you, too, Joe Bob. I knew you'd understand."

"Not too close. I could suffocate."

(If you're a woman and you're reading this right now, *please* don't kill me.)

In other words, they don't think this is funny. Better to avoid the subject altogether.

Okay, let's get to the only part of the date most of you *animals* care about: the nookie at the end. I've got some bad news for you in the nineties:

They're acting like they don't *enjoy it* anymore. It's that old fifties thing come back to haunt us. We've got to actually *perform* to get anywhere *close* to the Beautyrest.

Somebody sent me a copy of this new book, *How to Get the Women You Desire into Bed,* by Ross Jeffries, which guarantees that if you follow the steps in the book, any woman will start whimpering like a wounded puppy every time you enter the room.

I realize you probly already have your own copy, but I have some additional advice caused by a recent experience with Wanda Bodine.

See, the whole point of the book is you have to become a *manly* man. You go out there on the dating scene and start *telling* these women what they need. You say things like, "If you wanna date me, be on time for dinner and keep your mouth *shut* about your problems. And get a new haircut."

So the principle of the book is that if you say things to women that *should* cause you to end up in the hospital, they'll fall in love with you instead.

The first night I put this idea into practice, I was planning on taking Wanda Bodine to my favorite night spot, Grapevine All-Star Lanes and Cocktails, and when we got there, this guy named Charles, who drives the golf cart they sell beer out of, made a disparaging remark about Wanda's hot pants being fire-engine red.

Actually, they were *not* fire-engine red. They were candy-apple red. After all, Wanda is a league bowler. But that's not the point. The point is that I decided to deal with this situation in a *manly* manner.

So I beat Charles up.

And Wanda was very impressed. It was *working*. She said, "You've never been so chivalrous before."

So I use this technique for ten minutes and already she notices my chivalrousness.

Next thing you know, we're locked in deadly battle with a bowling team called the Dancing Asthmatics, and the Dancing Asthmatics are up by about a hundred pins, and I'm thinking, "If there's one thing a woman can't stand, it's a man who can't *bowl* with authority."

So I beat up Waldo Whitaker, who has a 174 average. Waldo never could get back the full use of his right arm, and so in the final and deciding game, he only bowled a 42.

And now Wanda is *very* impressed.

"I like a man who *takes* what he *wants*," she said breathlessly.

I revived her and reminded her to take more breaths.

Finally, I've got Wanda just exactly where I want her. We're in the Eleventh Frame cocktail lounge, about to do some serious Whitney Houston body-grinding on the dance floor, when in walks this guy called Hugh "the Hunk" Hofstatter. And I knew he was gonna be trouble.

He walks up to Wanda, steps right in front of me, and says "Who's the dork?"

So, as you can see, the situation is a little complicated, because he's not talking to me, he's talking to Wanda. And Wanda says, "He's not a dork."

And I was all pumped up from reading the book, so I said "I'm the dork. I mean, I'm *not* a dork, but I *am* the dork for the purposes of this conversation, because you referred to me as a dork, and to simplify matters I will acknowledge that you were referring to me when you used the d-word."

So Hofstatter just grins at me and then he says to Wanda, "What if the two of us *fight* for the right to take you home?"

And I'm thinking "What kind of ridiculous deal is this from the thirteenth century? Fight to take her home?" And I'm laughing.

And then Wanda says, "I think that would be *wonderful.*"

And it was then, at that moment, that I realized what I had to do.

"You can have this bimbo," I told him.

Women invented this macho stuff. Do you realize this? *We* get beat up, and *they* enjoy it.

Whew! That was close. So we can get rid of *that* book. No date is worth dying for, or, in my opinion, even getting your elbow bruised. In fact, I already think we men do too much in the name of getting a little nookie. It's never *that great,* is it? And then, after we get it, we're never quite sure whether we wanted what we got.

Do you know what I'm talking about?

And now science has *proven* that we don't even *want* sex that much. You know, every time I start to feel like I'm halfway normal, some dunderhead psychologist comes out with new theories about what's wrong with my Aardvarkus Whingdingus, if you know what I mean and I think you do.

Have you heard this latest one? It's that when two people get married, it causes 70 percent of the *males* in the relationship to get so sexually bored after two years that 70 percent of the *females* go around *begging* to make the sign of the three-pronged flying squirrel, if you know what I mean and of *course* you do.

"It's the *woman* who wants it more often," this psychologist guy says.

Now I find this hard to believe, because what have we men been told our *entire* lives?

"You're such an *animal!* Don't you ever think of *anything else?*"

Is this one of those Female Things that we don't understand? Is this some way of manipulating us into buying a thirty-buck dinner at Reynaldo's Le Brasserie Wursthaus? Because I have to admit, if it is, then I've been falling for it my whole dang life.

They have a name for this thing: Desire Discrepancy. At least this is what they call it when the woman says "Yes yes yes" but the man says "No way, José Feliciano."

When it's the other way around, and the man wants nookie but his Significant Other doesn't, they have another name for it: Date Rape.

Anyhow, the way you deal with Desire Discrepancy is you call a meeting and you "talk through the issue in a friendly manner. Try to identify what's wrong. Is there a basic discrepancy in sex drive or has an emotional conflict caused one of you to lose interest?"

Let's see now, how would this go?

"Ravish me," she says.

"Well, now, let's talk about that," he says. "When you say 'ravish,' do you mean *sexually?*"

"Now! I need you! I want you!"

"Let me analyze the signals I'm getting from you," he says. "If I didn't know you better, I'd say you were making an indecent proposal."

"Yes! Yes! I'm indecent! I'm *very very* indecent!"

"Could it be that you're crying out for help? Could it be that you *think* you want sex, but what you really want is some form of emotional reassurance?"

"No! No! I want *sex! Please!* Sex! Sex! Sex!"

"I guess we'll just have to seek therapy and counseling," the man says.

Is this really happening? In America?

Or are couples just doing it the way we do it in Texas:

"Do you want me?"

"Yep."

"Have at it."

Now isn't this a lot more civilized?

Women Are Crazy:
Get Used to It

Okay, forget dating. That doesn't work. We've got to address a more fundamental problem: Women have lost it.

I'm not talking about a gradual thing, either. It happened about midway through 1978. It was over before we realized it. Collectively, one entire nation of females went off their nut.

And here's the most amazing part of it: Most of them decided they wanted to be men.

In the next three or four chapters—the "women are nuts" chapters—I'm gonna *prove* this, so hang in there with me. And I'm gonna start with this proposition:

Women have *no idea* what they want, because, if they did, they'd never ask for the things men already have.

First example: female executives.

The old fight about "women in the boardroom" is starting up again.

No way we can allow women in the boardroom.

Never work.

I'll tell you why it'll never work:

Let's say there's a meeting of the board of directors of the Hugely Important Multi-National Synthetic Petro-Fabric Corporation. There are eighteen directors and six officers, all men. They're all in midtown Manhattan, sitting around a table hand-carved from seven acres of Amazon rain forest. A man named Bowker is serving them Indian tea and smoked-salmon sandwiches.

The chairman opens the meeting by calling on the president for his report.

The president talks about the recent acquisition of a Japanese tool maker and how it's "one of the proudest moments in the history of Petro-Fabric, with a very promising future as a profit center."

The president sits down, and the vice president in charge of international trade makes a speech about how "we couldn't have carried off this merger without the hard work and dedication of Herb, Willis, Frank, and Ryan."

Herb, Willis, Frank, and Ryan all smile and nod:

"Great job, Stan. Way to work those trenches."

"I guess after all those trips to Japan, Stan, you probably know how to play golf by now."

Hardy har har. Everybody laughs. Hardy har har.

And then every single person at the table, as he reports on whatever the hell it is he's supposed to report on, puts in his two cents about what a "wonderful opportunity" the new merger is, or what "bright profit prospects" the new merger gives the company, or blah blah blah, even if the guy is only in charge of the building's air-conditioning system and so he doesn't give one big diddly-squat about the Japanese merger. It's part of the ritual. It's what you do at these meetings. It preserves the idea that we are *in control.* We *set* a goal, we *strove* for the goal, we *achieved* the goal.

Now let's put a woman into this little scenario. Let's call her Gretchen. Gretchen is the new board member.

Stan gets up and makes the same identical speech. Gretchen listens intently to what he's saying, and she *actually tries to understand the meaning of the words.* This is her first mistake.

"Stan, about that Japanese merger," Gretchen will say. "Isn't that the deal that got started because that kid Bill Collins down in the mail room clipped an article out of the *Wall Street Journal* and told his supervisor 'We should buy this company'? Isn't that funny, how such a huge success could happen to us almost by *accident?*"

Gretchen chuckles. Nobody else chuckles.

"I don't remember how it got started," Stan replies lamely. "You may very well be right."

And then someone will be forced to say, "You know, it was Jack in Acquisitions that *really* got the ball rolling, made those initial calls. Let's have a big hand for Jack!"

Now they're laughing again. Now the awkwardness is broken. You see, Gretchen failed to realize that things that happen by accident are *not allowed* in board rooms. Jack did it, or Stan did it, or Herb did it, or Frank did it, or *we* did it, but never *ever* does it "just happen."

Women don't understand this.

Another thing women don't understand is that when the chairman is talking, he is not throwing out propositions or asking for help in formulating his plan, or even *informing* the board of anything. He is *chanting* a ritualistic mantra. It's like an African ceremony. Even the jokes are this way. Most of the jokes have been told *hundreds* of times before, but everyone *looks forward* to them, hangs on them, laughs at them.

The chairman says, "Did I ever tell you what happened to us that time in Cleveland when Fred Findiman lost the slides for the Goodyear presentation?"

And Gretchen, if she's not thinking, is gonna say, "Yes, you told that story at the last board meeting. That's a *very* funny story."

And Gretchen thinks she's said something polite, but suddenly everyone at the boardroom table is staring at their shoes, and Gretchen is thinking, "Didn't anybody else *hear* the story last time?"

Or maybe the chairman is going on and on about the nobility of the new direct-mail data base, and Gretchen is listening to this guy and watching him, and she can't stop staring at his ears, because he has *giant ear hairs* all tangled up in there like a potato that's been left in a glass of water for three days. And it doesn't matter what the guy says. From now on, for the rest of his life, whenever she meets him, Gretchen will know him as The Man with Giant Ear Hairs. She can't help it. How can you take a person with giant ear hairs seriously?

And God forbid Gretchen should be in the room when there's a *real* crisis going on.

"From what Operations is telling me, we spilled about one-point-eight million barrels of heavy crude near the Great Barrier Reef of Australia. But we have a team of managers en route to the site at this time. Our emergency procedures have been put in place. We expect to have it all cleaned up in about two weeks, with little or no damage to wildlife. What we've got to guard against is the kind of alarmist talk going on in the news media."

And everybody is nodding, circling the wagons, sucking in guts, saying, "Yes, that's the correct position. Tell em, Ron!"

And Gretchen can't stand it. She says, "Are we going to *apologize* to those people? I hope we're not just ignoring them. This should *never* have happened. This is *awful.*"

And then the president has to say something like, "Gretchen, in our business, accidents are inevitable."

"Yes, and when they happen you say *'We screwed up'!*"

"Gretchen, you can't say 'We screwed up.' We're fixing the problem."

"That doesn't matter. People want to know we're genuinely *sorry,* not that we're rushing around like loonies."

"It's a P.R. matter, hon."

You see what a can of worms this is? Every corporation, like every husband, is a demi-god who *must* believe certain things about himself even if he *and* the wife *and* everybody else knows they're totally untrue. The whole structure depends on understanding this peculiar religion and respecting it.

But there's my point: Gretchen is never gonna make it to the boardroom in the first place. Gretchen will spend ten minutes in that place and book the next ship to Bora Bora. Gretchen couldn't *stand* to hang out with these guys.

So what we have instead is the New Corporate Woman, that extremely rare type of female who, we've decided, *is* qualified for the boardroom. You've probly seen em around the office. They're reserved but cheerful. They wear "sensible" clothing. They don't have much to say. When they're around men, they smile a lot. They're always on the *verge* of contributing something, but then they change their minds. You'll notice the expression on their faces. It's the same one you'll find on the faces of battered wives.

These women are okay in the boardroom, and I'm sure they'll go far, because they've managed to become *male* in their minds.

I'm right, aren't I?

But that's not the only thing that happened that night in 1978 when all American women went bonkers. Because a lot of the *older* women, the pre–Sexual Revolution honeys, *also* checked themselves into Bellevue. These were the women who suddenly decided they'd missed out on something by being born before 1950 and now it was time to *catch up.*

Here's a disgusting example. One of my favorite great-aunts, Vera Glasscock, on the Bardwell side of the East Texas Briggses, just got a job working in the Men's Billfold Department of J. C.

Penney's in Fort Worth, and I've been put in charge of watching her so she doesn't commit any indecent public acts or otherwise embarrass the family.

Vera is the only eighty-nine-year-old woman with a full-frontal photograph in the *Texas Connection* swingers magazine.

We told Vera it's not gonna work, there's no such thing as eighty-nine-year-old swingers, and even if there *is* such a thing, they *still* don't wanna see any nude pictures of her, but Vera believes that after fifty-five years of daily goat's-milk skin treatments, she has the face, body, and personality of a twenty-nine-year-old. That's what she'll tell you. "I have the face, body, and personality of a twenty-nine-year-old," she'll tell you. "Billy Tompkins said so."

And I told her, "Vera, Billy Tompkins also *died* in 1955."

Also, I'm the guy that has to deal with the *Texas Connection* editorial staff when they call me up. "Please, Joe Bob, make her take the ad out," they say. "We'll pay *her* money. We're getting letters from people that think it's a picture of a suffering animal being used for medical research. We don't want the animal-rights people on our backs."

And so I tried to talk to Vera once or twice, but she said, "They advertise *free* photos for unattached female swingers, and by God I'm unattached, and by God I'm female, and by God I'm a swinger."

"Well, could you at least tone down the copy a little bit? Take out the stuff about the garden hoes?"

"Joe Bob, I'm surprised at you! I thought you were one of the more *liberal* Briggses!"

"I am, Vera, but it makes people think you're a tropical plant."

You can't reason with the woman. She's the most sexually active eighty-nine-year-old on the planet. And so now what happens, but she goes and she gets a *job*. And she not only gets a *job,* she gets one where she's been trying to get a job her whole life—J. C. Penney's Men's Billfold Department—and she did it for one reason. She's gonna *snag* one of those guys before he knows what hit him. *And* she gets to see what's in his billfold first.

So I drove out to Fort Worth to try to talk to her. But when I got there it was already too late. She had some of the finer cowhide models *out* of their cellophane-covered billfold gift boxes, and what do you think she was doing with em? She was *removing* the photo of Vic Damone, and she was *replacing* it with *her* picture.

And it was the one from the *Texas Connection* magazine!

"Vera, I've got two choices. I can wait here till you pass one of those billfolds to a customer and J. C. Penny's fires your hiney and the Fort Worth Vice Squad comes in here and hauls you off to the Texas State Institute for the Feeble-Minded. Or you can *reassemble* those cellophane covers *right this minute* and *get those billfolds back into their original condition*. The choice is yours."

But right at that moment I had to stop talking, because a well-dressed, gray-haired gentleman ambled up to the sales counter and said, "Excuse me, but I'm looking for something in lizard."

"Natural lizard or imitation lizard?" Vera said.

"I'm looking for a lizard that . . . er . . . " He hesitated.

"Go ahead," she told him, "I think I can help you."

"I would like to speak to the lady who . . . uh . . . it has to do with a photograph . . . "

"You looking for the Lizard Lady, honey?"

"You mean it's *you!* I want seven more pictures, and I want you to have dinner with me. Sorry, I didn't recognize you with your clothes on."

"It's all right, hon, happens all the time."

I can tell that Vera's gonna soil the Briggs family reputation all over North Texas again.

I'm telling you, it happened about halfway through 1978.

A Few Words About the Hooter

Here's another thing that happened to women when they went crazy—this breast thing. Three hundred years from now this will be a trivia question:

In the years 1980 to 1992, in the United States of America, millions of women had their chests sliced open and a bag of jelly inserted inside. True or false?

And *nobody* will get the right answer.

Isn't this the weirdest goldurn thing you've ever heard somebody do to herself?

I'm sure you know what I'm talking about—how the old Food and Drug Administration had to finally *outlaw* fake breasts.

They say they're dangerous. They say they can go haywire on you. Last year they had a bunch of hearings in Washington where women showed up with breasts that had *shifted* on em. The doctor put em in one way, then they woke up one morning with a chest that was all catty-wampus, one pointing at Alaska and the other one pointing at Key West.

Sure, there were other women who showed up with stunt

breasts that had done their job properly for up to *thirty years,* and they were *proud* of those hooters. Their chests swelled with pride. And silicone.

But Ralph Nader had noticed that more than *two million* women in America have had surgical augmentation of their bazoomas. Did you realize this? We're talking the entire female populations of Arkansas and Mississippi put together have walked into a hospital somewhere and said, "Go ahead, cut on me a while, just make sure I walk out of here with a set of headlamps the size of Wisconsin."

And so Ralph Nader decides that some of these artificial dinglebobbers just *might* be a little *dangerous,* especially at high speeds, and so he does a few tests on em. Ralph took your typical silicone-gel baggie—it's this little floating Jell-O mold that the surgeon plants in the middle of your breast like a turnip—and he threw it up against a brick wall like a dodge-ball to see if he could break it. And then they made giant fifty-pound silicone implants and used em for bean-bag chairs for six months, to see if they'd hold their shape. And then he studied these complaints from women who said that they'd go get the surgery, get a new set of P.T. boats, be *perfectly happy* with the results—but then what happens?

Three months later, they *freeze up* on you. All of a sudden you hear this cracking noise, and your garbonzas go into freeze-frame, and you got a couple of thirty-pound icebergs hanging off the front of your chest. You can't move em with a block and tackle. You touch em and it feels like somebody welded an iron skillet under your skin. And then you gotta start doing this daily massage therapy on your flopdoodles, where you try to "break down" the hard material, and if *that* doesn't work, you gotta go *back* to the doctor's office and let him do the job with a Louisville Slugger. Let's not dwell on it.

Of course, your reverse problem is when you get *droopers.*

You get the new size of Balboas you were looking for, but they just hang off your chest like the skin on an elephant. For temporary help the doctor can issue you a set of water wings, which you can turn around and wear on your chest under the underperforming Winnebagos, but sooner or later you're gonna have to find some permanent support, like a "flesh trestle," or your dreaded Golden Gate suspension surgery.

In other words, women were starting to realize that there's way too much we don't know about surgical enlargement of your Fujiyamas, and, until we do know the answers, you'd best leave small enough alone. On the other hand, when those hearings began, some of em also realized that if you're *really* desperate and you're *sure* that sooner or later you're gonna wanna freshen up the old Dueling Banjos, then you'd better go ahead and do it before the official ban begins and they run out of imitation breasts at the big mazonga factories in the Grand Tetons. These companies were getting desperate, so they started discounting the price—so you could go in with a friend, get two new chests for the price of one, things like that.

So there was actually a *run* on fake boobies. But that was certainly better than the alternative—selling all our surplus silicone baggies to ignorant people in the Third World. Sure, there are a lot of Bangladeshi women who wake up every morning and gnash their teeth because they're too poor to possess forty-two-inch howitzers, but if they suddenly became available, how could we know they wouldn't be trading one affliction for another? Three months after getting a new set of Pia Zadoras, they might accidentally put a child's eye out. If you're gonna own these things, you've got to know how to use them.

I, for one, don't want that on my conscience.

Then the committee that was studying the artificial zeppelins decided that, no, they wouldn't ban em, because it was an infringement on the personal liberty to have anything hanging off your chest that you wanted. But then a whole bunch of women complained, and doctors testified, and—*whap*—six months later they reversed themselves and outlawed those little suckers (actually those *big* suckers), because they got all this testimony from women whose chests look like relief maps of Switzerland. The biggest doctors in America weighed the comparative benefits—namely, huge gazongas—and the comparative risks—namely, that your insides might turn all mooshy and make you sick for the rest of your life—and decided that you ladies have got to stop boosting those loblollies with artificial boob extenders.

So this is gonna be very interesting.

Now, every time we see a nekkid woman in the movies, we're gonna be thinking, "Lemme see now, how old is she? I just *wonder* if she had those made up special during that historic period between 1980 and 1992 when you could buy hooters off the rack?"

And people will have arguments about it.

"Naw, she's too young for that. She couldn't of been more than fourteen years old when Garbonza Prohibition started."

And then all the people who were *thinking* about having fake bra-busters put in *right before the ban* will be kicking themselves for the rest of their lives. "Yeah, *sure* she has a better figure than I do, but I didn't have the money to get the kind of bronskis I needed—and then it was *too late.* In fact, my surgery was scheduled for the following Wednesday. And you *wonder* why I'm *bitter!*"

And then the women who *did* get em before the ban will be so goldang proud of em: "Honey, they aren't making *these* babies anymore!"

You know what happened the last time we had Prohibition. The *mob* stepped in and sold liquor anyway.

So I'm sure Gotti and his guys are trying to figure this one out right now. Pretty soon we'll have illegal fake-breast distilleries all up and down the East Coast. In five years, every major city will have breast-easys, with dark smoke-filled back rooms where you can buy all the bags of silicone you can carry home. Evil back-alley doctors will implant them, using *coat hangers,* and . . . well, maybe not, I don't know.

Anyhow, don't you think there should have been a warning period or something? An announcement, like, "Nobody gets any fake breasts after October 1." Something like that? Then every woman who ever wanted fake breasts or thought she might *need* em sometime in the future, and especially our hardworking topless dancers who are sagging a little and might like to add five or six years to their careers—all of these women, tax-paying citizens, could have rushed out and gotten the breasts they deserve. Or they would have had a *chance* to anyhow.

But the ban came suddenly, without warning, choking off self-expression like a corset that's four sizes too small. That was cruel. That was uncalled-for. What do you think these women are, pieces of *meat?*

The Lesbo Boom

I first noticed the Lesbo Boom about five years ago. Actually, it started out when women started talking about their "biological clocks" all the time. I know this has nothing to do, per se, ipso facto, dipsy doodle, with lesbianism, but hang with me a minute, and I'll explain it.

It started when Wanda Bodine told me that since she's so fat, she might as well get pregnant. It would be a good time to do it, she said, especially since she has her law degree now and so she'd be able to figure out how to dump that baby in day care after two, three weeks and force somebody else to pay for it.

"My biological clock has done run around the dial three times," is the way she put it.

None of this babbling about being pregnant bothered me, particularly, until she started rubbing up against me in the line at Wyatt's Cafeteria and saying stuff like "I just bought a new Posturepedic and pretty soon I'll have money for sheets."

Then it occurred to me—she's gonna need a *male individual* to carry this off.

I don't know if you've ever met any of the Bodine sisters, but they get em a husband for five, six weeks, use him long enough to plant some seeds where it counts, and then tell him "You, Dwayne, are not fulfilling my potential as a modern woman, you never pick up your socks, and we have nothing in common."

Course, by then they do have something in common. Dwayne just doesn't find out till seven months later when she calls him up about "sharing the expenses of our child."

I never did understand this until Wanda and her sister Doreen explained it to me one night. I was thinking all my life all a woman wanted was a man she could manipulate into marrying her. What they really want is a man they can manipulate into giving em *babies*. I thought it was *husbands* they wanted, but it's *babies*. This is the thing for the woman of the nineties. Get rid of that turkey just as soon as he's done the *one job* in the poor sucker's life that he can't get fired from, then boot his hiney out of there before he does something stupid like *admit he's the father*. That gets you into all kinds of legal problems like being forced to run the kid out to his house on weekends when you don't have a date.

Anyhow, the Bodine sisters have had nine babies now—and they're all named Bodine except for little Raul. They call him "Raul Bodino" because nobody'd believe it if you called him plain Bodine. So I think you can see what's going on here. The only reason I bring it up is that I don't give a flip, personally, I know how to protect my personal integrity in the Wyatt's Cafeteria line and not go ape just cause some 260-pound baby-making machine flashes a little thigh while she's shoving a tray full of lemon meringue through the check-out line, but many of you reading this book might not have ever met the Bodine sisters and so when Wanda shows up, you'll be dead meat. After all, she's *real* good looking for a gal that looks like she oughta have an apple in her mouth.

Okay, so that's the story on the Bodine sisters, and about five years ago I first started writing about em and pointing out how Wanda and Doreen no longer marry the men they choose to breed with. But when I was writing about this, I thought this was a *new thing,* invented by the Bodine sisters so they could treat men like old dirty dishrags, score some sperm from us, and then hoist our hineys into the street before we know what we've hatched. All these women are *panicked* about their goldurn biological clock turning their fallopian tubes into a pumpkin.

Anyhow, some friends of mine out in California started sending me these articles about the "lesbian baby boom." Maybe you're not familiar with the lesbian baby boom. At first I thought it was true what we've thought all along: people in California came here from another planet, and all the people born there since World War II are space-alien science experiments that divide like amoebas. Either that or else all these lesbians have been having a lot of sex with one another and trying *real* hard.

But it turns out that the lezzies are showing up at the sperm bank and saying "Gimme one of them test tubes with some of that icky stuff in it that *men* have." And then they get em a lesbo sex partner to frizz up her hair like Anne Murray, and they figure that when the little frog-faced booger is born, he'll never know the difference. They can name him something like Jeremiah—nope, too sexist—how about Noah?—nope, they'd laugh at him when he goes to Montessori School. I've got it! Jessie! Could be a boy. Could be a girl. The perfect name for the kid who's gonna wake up one day and think, "You know, there seem to be way too many sets of panty hose around this house."

This stuff is great, though. Soon as I heard about it, I ran over to tell Wanda that all she needs is Artificial Spermatization. "You know," I told her, "it's like they do with racehorses. You want Secretariat's genes? The vet takes some of them Secretariat genes, sticks em in a hypo, and then he makes sure they get to their destination. Eleven months later, Secretariat doesn't know *which one* belongs to him. It's the exact same thing with humans, only you need to start you out on a strong lesbian relationship in order to give the resulting Bodine child a strong and supportive environment."

"I don't need a lesbian," she said. "I got Doreen around the house all day."

"Doreen doesn't count. Your own sister? That would be perverted!"

"Oh," Wanda said.

Anyway, you probly know where this is leading. You've probly read about it already. From that point forward I became fascinated with the Lesbo Movement, and I stayed hot on the trail of every new lesbian trend, right up until I attended the National Lesbian Conference in the summer of 1991.

By the way, I wanna thank everyone for the cards, letters, flowers, and telegrams you sent me during those long few weeks while I was recuperating at Parkland Hospital in Dallas.

In retrospect, I *knew* I shouldn't have attended the National Lesbian Conference. You warned me. You told me to stay away. Even Wanda Bodine tried to protect me. She said, "Joe Bob, you ever seen what a two-hundred-and-fifty-pound woman with a burr haircut can do to the human pelvis?"

But I told her, "Wanda, I'm a reporter. I've got to check these things out."

And so I volunteered to go to the big convention in Atlanta with the Texas delegation. After all, I told em, with that many women in one bus, who was gonna *drive?*

That was when I got the first sprained elbow from being sat on by Wendy "the Mattress" Stubbs. She put her knees between my shoulder blades and twisted my arm and wouldn't let go until I yelled "Aunt!"

IRON JOE BOB

A couple days later I showed up with my notebook and tape recorder at the Handicapped Jewish Lesbian Caucus. They weren't gonna let me in, so I faked the guards out by putting on a dress and riding in a motorized wheelchair and saying the word *schlemiel* a lot. I had one of those little black beanies on my head, which is what gave me away, because I didn't realize that handicapped Jewish lesbians don't wear those little black beanies.

This one-armed woman named Shirley Steinberg challenged me. She said, "You're not *Jewish*. No self-respecting lesbian Jew would wear a yammakuller like that."

And I tried to fake it. I said, "Well, I realize that, but I thought that since Jewish *men* get to wear em, it was only right that Jewish *women* who *look like men* should get to wear em, too . . . "

And she was about to buy this when she noticed I was wearing a pink chiffon taffeta party dress from J. C. Penney's, and she said, "I don't even think you're a lesbian."

And I couldn't *believe* I'd done that. *Of course*. I should have worn a polyester pants suit. I could of got away with the whole deal.

Anyway, that's how I got the multiple rib fractures, from being kicked out the door by three ladies named Frank, Steve, and Mumbles the Molester.

I don't know if you read much about the convention, but it got really interesting around the third day, when all the lesbos started beating one another up. The Elderly Lesbians got mad at the Lesbian Avocado Farmers, and the Lesbians of Color got ticked off because there weren't enough Puerto Rican–Arab Lesbians admitted to the convention floor, and then some Overeating Lesbians who were dressed up in black leather *Star Trek* costumes ambushed some Lesbian Marines and crushed one gal's skull for being a tool of the imperialist American military forces. And then, of course, there was the Dykes on Bikes circus act that had to be canceled because the unicycles they were using were made at a factory in Poland that discriminates against lesbian porpoise trainers.

Finally, on the last day of the convention, I managed to get inside by wearing my normal clothes but passing myself off as an eighteen-year-old girl who had taken a *lot* of steroids. *It worked!* I should have done this right from the beginning.

And so, when I finally got a firsthand look at what was going on, they were having a debate between the representative of Native American Lesbians, Babs Stumbling Buffalo, and the representative of the Radical African-American Nuclear-War-Now Lesbians of Inner Detroit, whose name was Mahogany Sims. And they were yelling and screaming at one another. Babs was claiming that the American Indian male was the most disgusting, sexist, no-good, abusive sorry excuse for a human being in the universe. But Mahogany said that, no, if you'd ever met her second ex-husband Kaleem "the Scream" Akim, then you would know that she had no choice but to chop his body into thirty-seven pieces and mail him to Armour Beef in Chicago. And when Mahogany mentioned actual *crimes,* that set off the United Lesbian Convicts Who Shouldn't Have Gone to Prison Except Some Worthless Man Sold Drugs in Their House, and they started chanting "Free all lesbian prisoners! Free all lesbian prisoners!"

And so I felt the situation was about to get out of hand—call me an idiot, but I decided to step in—and so I asked for permission to speak, and, after everybody quieted down, I stood up and I said, "Y'all would feel a whole lot better if you'd take two Midol."

That's how I got the brain injuries.

They say, with physical therapy, I could have a normal life again within two or three years.

Now, right after I went to the lesbo convention that summer, even *before* I was fully recovered, I started reporting on my lesbian experiences in various American newspapers. And some of the lesbos did *not* like it.

They are Woman, hear them roar.

So I'd like to take this opportunity to apologize to the lesbos of America for any remarks they considered vile and degrading. They were not intended in that spirit.

Evidently there were some lesbians in San Francisco and Aspen who wrote in to the paper demanding that I be strapped into a leather corset and flogged with a punji stick. Of course, when they found out this is one of my secret fantasies, they withdrew the offer.

Let there be no mistake about it. I respect the right of lesbians to do any disgusting thing they want to with their bodies and/or farm implements. After all, this is America. In fact, I would like to make the following public statements, for the benefit of those lesbians who were offended:

1. I am opposed to the random killing, mutilation, and torture of women, unless it's necessary to the plot.

2. Your body belongs to you, except when you sell it.

3. Martina Navratilova is my favorite Romanian.

4. I didn't mean to imply that all lesbians look like men. After all, some men wear dresses.

5. Many of the lesbos who wrote in said I shouldn't be abbreviating "lesbians" with the term "lesbos." I was merely using the ancient Greek term, which originated on the Isle of Lesbos, home of Sappho and other important bohemian females. Since the modern lesbian movement seems to have forgotten this, I will no longer use either "lesbo" or the

corrupt Latin term "lesbian," but the more neutral Mesopotamian term for any woman of this persuasion:

Naugahyde Sofa Woman.

6. I think Birkenstock sandals are extremely attractive on a size 14 foot.

7. Several of the professional . . . er . . . Naugahyde Sofa Women—sorry, but it'll take a while for me to get used to it—several of these people wrote in to say that there were certain jokes that just should *not* be made about . . . uh . . . *those people,* and that anyone who would make those jokes should be banned from print. Up till now, there have only been two groups that continually argue for actually *removing* unpopular opinions from newspapers and TV—the fundamentalists and the feminists. So I need clarification. Is this a *branch* of the feminists, or should we create a third category? But if you gals have been meeting with the Reverend Donald Wildmon and the Americans for Decency to discuss strategies for getting rid of me, I would like to see a transcript and a seating chart. I'll pay up to $24.95.

8. I read the book *The White Goddess,* even the footnotes in Welsh, and I agree that we should all worship the One Great Big-Breasted Earth Mother. In my dreams her name is Monique.

9. The public image of lesbians is all wrong. Most people think of them as big fat razor-headed snarling wolf-women in biker jackets with hairy armpits and stinky flabby arms. This is completely unfair. Most of them look like Helen Reddy.

10. I'm thinking of becoming a lesbian myself. It's a nineties thing.

I hope this has cleared up the misunderstanding.

Men Are More Crazy Than Women

Men went crazy around August of 1984. I don't exactly what caused it, but it happened fast and it happened to everybody at once. We still haven't gotten over it. We still go around looking for presidential candidates and preachers who *haven't* gone crazy, and then we get all hacked off when it turns out they don't exist.

I think the first guy to go totally bonkers in public was Jim Bakker.

I'll never forget the day I first heard the news about Jimbo. We held an all-night prayer vigil down at Church Under the Rock, and thirty-seven ministers of the ever-lovin gospel came down to give their testimony and kick dirt on Jim Bakker and the PTL Club cause Jimbo told everybody how he got some on the side and then paid $115,000 for it later and now he lost his teevee show cause Jerry Falwell says he can't preach to millions of people anymore cause he has Sin oozin out of his pores and so he has to go to the Betty Ford Brain Therapy Center with Tammy and the kids and figure out why he's the only man in the history of the universe that ever diddled around and embarrassed the brethren.

And I had to stand up for Jimbo at the prayer meetin and say, "Hey! Hold it! Wait just a goldurn minute! Whoa! Can we have *just a little* slack here?"

And the Reverend T. Sullivan Dembo of the Epileptic Sons of the Two Living Gods allowed me to speak, cause the Reverend Dembo is so charismatic that his church don't just speak in tongues, they speak in *noses,* and so he lets anybody speak, specially if they might fall down on the floor and start twitchin their elbows.

And I told this lynch mob to just hold it just a minute, if we'd just put everything in perspective, it's real crystal clear what kind of message we wanna send to Reverend Jimbo. That message had to be loving, kind, compassionate—to him, and to his Lipstick Lizard wife, too. Here was my message:

"Jim, son, listen up. A hundred and fifteen thousand is way too much to pay for nookie. That's not good stewardship with the Lord's money. We think you're bein' a little extravagant. For example, the highest recorded amount ever paid by a Methodist minister was two hundred and fifty dollars. We're not saying you can't pay *more* than that, but let's keep it in the ballpark."

Here's a quick reference guide to the open market, in case this ever comes up again (all prices indexed by confidential surveys taken in Murfreesboro, Tennessee, home of *Sword of the Lord* magazine):

Average nookie price, Mormon executive high priest: $3,000.

(Jim, you can see right here, you're *way over* the limit. That's a difference of more than $100,000.)

Average nookie price, Church of Christ: $2,000.

Pentecostal: $1,000.

Southern Babtist: $850.

Northern Babtist: $50.

Catholic priest: $750.

IRON JOE BOB

Episcopal: $500.

Methodist: $250.

Presbyterian: $50.

Unitarian: $5.

Jim, to tell you the truth, we've never even heard of a *layman* payin $115,000, and so I hope you've learned your lesson. In the future, *always get a receipt.* God loves you, and I love you, but the girl that charges $115,000 don't love you, Jim. I'm sorry.

Okay, now come on back and do the show. We miss you.

Unfortunately, Jimbo ended up in the Crossbar Hotel and never *did* come back and do the show, but I didn't give up on him, like many of my so-called Christian brothers did. A few weeks after it happened I went out West to the Betty Ford Center for Screwin Your Head Back On Straight, and I asked Jim and Tammy Faye and the family to get down on their knees with me and spill their guts and stop this vicious media attack on the sanctity of their sexual relations, and then we said a little prayer together about church secretaries and it went something like this:

"I'm sorry, God, for payin $265,000 of Your money for somethin that, let's face it, was worth about a quarter, especially since I only admitted to paying $115,000. We could of used that money for another log-flume ride at Jesusland Amusement Park and had some left over to fly in some white yuppie gospel singers that play the accordion and sing through their nose. Tammy could of bribed somebody to bring back her Christian recording career. We could of even fed the starvin people that hover around the gates of our Palm Springs home, saying 'Wash your Rolls for a five.' It was the Devil that crept down into the evil part of my body and said to me, 'What a pair of Methuselahs on that palomino! Let's play Dunkin' Donuts in a waterbed!' And you know what the worst part of it is, Your Angry Highness, Sir? It lasted only twenty seconds."

Then Jimbo and me had a discussion about whether he

could get some Brownie points from God on the basis of it was *only* for twenty seconds that the Sin lasted, but we decided we better not press our luck by prayin too much in one day, and so then we planned a series of statements to the press, giving out the *real* facts about the situation as they were revealed to me by Jim himself, and so that's why I'm takin the time right now to set the record straight:

Numero Uno: Jimmy Swaggart told on me.

Numero Two-o: Jerry Falwell took all my toys and wouldn't give em back.

Numero Three-o: Honey Hahn, the church secretary, did everything to aggravate me and she didn't tell it right.

Numero Four-o: My answer to Honey Hahn is "Did not, did not."

Numero Five-o: Oral Roberts was the only one who was nice to me.

Numero Six-o: I get to keep all my money. It's my money. I get to keep it.

Numero Seven-o: Nyah nyah nyah.

I hope this puts a perspective on everything, and now we can leave this persecuted Christian man and his family alone in peace.

What's the deal with preachers, though? We had just barely gotten Jimbo and Tammy straightened out when along comes the *real* Pentecostals. There was one year when everywhere I went people were coming up to me, shoving *Penthouse* in front of my face so I could look at Debbie Murphree, the little tattooed gal that taught Jimmy Swaggart how to talk in tongues. Shame on you people, and thank you.

Then I kept seeing Deb on the talk-show circuit, explaining how all she ever wanted was the money, and I realized what the Man Upstairs was doing here. Deb, you may have noticed, has got a face on her like an ice-cream sandwich that's been run over by a Texaco truck. The most she could get out of Jimbo, one of the richest guys in Louisiana, was twenty bucks. So the prostitution thing wasn't working out for her. What's left?

God wanted *her* to have a giant church in Baton Rouge. After all, she's honest, she tells you the price in advance, and she's got enough spiritual knowledge to know you can't preach about what your body *ought* to be doing, cause as soon as you do, it's gonna do the opposite. She's a *born* evangelist.

I don't know what kind of papers might have to be shuffled around the Assembly of God grand wazoo headquarters in Springfield, Missouri, but I think they oughta just hand her the church keys tomorrow and let her rip.

The first text she could preach on would be *Penthouse* 19:11, 108–22. If there's anything guaranteed to make you give up sex for a week, this is it, especially page 115, which is so terrifying that when the *Penthouse*s were delivered to Billings, Montana, eighteen people had to be treated for acute stomach cramps.

"Yall looky here now," she could say to the congregation. "These are actual parts of my body. I know they don't *look* like parts of my body. I know they *look* like parts of a pork-sausage dinner that's been left up on the dashboard of your pickup in August. But someday, if you let your brain keep thinkin about trying to be holy, *you* will desire this. I hope you realize, we're talkin about something that drunk sexual deviates in Times Square would *refuse.* But *you* will want it, because *you* will be under the grip of the Swaggart Demon. It don't stop there either. After that you'll be 'cruising for pork' like a junkie *searching* for somebody that'll give you a quick fix. After that, you'll *beg* to be chained up and Jimmy-Deaned until you're unconscious. And finally, you'll start having indecent thoughts about Ralph the Diving Pig, the number one tourist attraction in San Marcos, Texas. Just think about it. Public scandal—and with a *celebrity* seen by ten million people a year. There's time, though. There's time to repent. Here, lemme help you."

And when she rips off her clothes, they'll all be down on their faces, beggin for mercy. Believe me, it can't miss.

But I don't wanna dump on Jimmy Swaggart any more than I dumped on Jimbo Bakker, because, in both cases, my point is that hundreds of thousands of men went crazy *together* at that exact time in history. I happen to be familiar with the Assembly of God tongue-talkin holy-rollin Pentecostal touchie-feelie regulations, 1983 revised code, that comes out of Springfield, Missouri, every year after a meeting of the Assembly of God Committee of Elders Who Only Have Sex with Their Wives but Never *Think* About It Before They Have It. As you know, this is the most powerful committee in the Pentecostal church, and it abides strictly by the following laws:

Numero Uno: Thou shalt not feel anything "down there."

Numero Two-o: If thou believes thou are about to feel something down there, due to the "Solid Gold" dancers coming on TV, thou shalt switch channels and repent by cold shower.

Numero Three-o: Thou shalt not covet thy neighbor's cleavage.

Numero Four-o: If said cleavage appears before thine eyes, due to heathen driving convertibles on the freeway, thou shalt avert thine eyes, crash thy vehicle, and quaff thy lust with a ball peen hammer.

Numero Five-o: If thy wife grows fat, thou shalt rejoice.

Numero Six-o: If thy wife wears white Spandex pedal pushers to the supermarket, thou shalt say "Thy will is large, Father."

Numero Seven-o: If thy wife appears as a balloon in the Macy's Thanksgiving Day Parade, thou shalt reap triple tithing and shout "Hallelu hallelujah hallelu."

Numero Eight-o: Thou shalt not tongue-talk on television.

Numero Nine-o: Thou shalt scrub thy body with Lifebuoy until it hurts.

Numero Ten-o: If thy lust destroys thy self-restraint and threatens thy church with scandal and a decrease in tithing, thou shalt use a VCR. (This is the one they got Jimmy on.)

Numero Eleven-o: If thou find thyself in peril, thou shalt never pay more than five dollars.

So, you see, this is what Jimmy was *doing,* being a good steward with the Lord's money, but what did it get him? Kicked out on his reverential hiney. It's enough to make me go back to being a Babtist, where you can do anything you want to *as long as you feel sorry about it later.*

That's enough on preachers. Those guys have been getting caught with peekaboo nookie for a hundred years. But then, right at the same point in history, all the *politicians* started rootin around like horny warthogs, too. And that's when I knew it was more than just a religious phenomenon.

The first one was Gary Hart and the *Tailgate* scandal. Remember? I guess it's too late now, but I had some evidence that would have gotten him off the hook. He could have been president by now. I followed Gary around for four days on the campaign trail, wrote down ever single time he took off his shorts, which, lemme say right here, is not a pleasant assignment, and established a relationship with Gary's traveling secretary, Trudi "Jugs" Fillmore. In fact, I got Trudi to type up all the results of the investigation.

April 17, 4:06 p.m., Fort Lauderdale, Florida: Gary boards his private yacht, *The Yankee Zipper,* for twenty-four hours of intensive speech preparation, accompanied only by his closest aides, twenty-seven-year-old makeup consultant Karen Funnel, and three fourteen-year-old Watusi girls. During this time Gary came in contact with no one else, except for the *Miami Herald* scuba team pressing their goggles up to his master bedroom porthole. *Nothing happened.*

April 18, 11:14 a.m., Key West, Florida: Gary steps off *The Yankee Zipper* and requests a two-hour shower. No one is seen entering or leaving the shower except Gary and a female Swedish masseuse weightlifter named Margrethe "Hands" Svenson. *Nothing happened.*

April 18, 5:15 p.m., Charleston, South Carolina: After a quick flight aboard his private campaign plane, *The Whangdoodle,* Gary addresses the state convention of the South Carolina Elks Clubs. Afterward, Gary rents an island off the coast and entertains 437 Elks with the help of *Whangdoodle* flight attendants. Again, nothing happened. Gary goes to bed early, about 7:15.

April 19, 9:45 a.m., Washington, D.C.: After stopping at the Charleston airport to buy ten giant stuffed teddy bears, Gary flies to the capital and enters a Georgetown condominium owned by Heather "the Human Pretzel" Funderburk, a longtime family friend. After two hours of nonstop campaigning, he leaves the condo and hands Heather a white envelope full of campaign donations for safekeeping. *Nothing happened.*

April 19, 3:15 p.m., Fairfax, Virginia: Gary is greeted by the entire Congressional delegation from the state of Vermont, meeting in executive session at Geno's Topless in suburban Washington for discussions on the maple-syrup industry. Gary watches a maple-syrup demonstration, but leaves early and stops at the Lincoln Memorial to pick up Rachel LeBrock, a researcher for the Department of Agriculture who agreed to take some specimens from Gary for lab analysis. She tells him the results were negative, and the two old friends spend the rest of the afternoon discussing holds used by the World Wrestling Federation. *Nothing happened.*

Nothin nothin nothin. I admit, I was trying to get somethin on the guy, but as far as I can see, he was railroaded into quitting by the *Miami Herald* nerds. Let's face it, if they're not gettin any, they don't want Gary to get any either.

Needless to say, once I exonerated Gary Hart with my investigation, the *Miami Herald* wanted revenge, and they were all over me for two weeks afterward. Finally I got tired of being harassed and abused and having my privates violated, and so I said, "Okay, you think you know somethin? You just follow *me* around for three days. I'm clean. You *try* to find somethin. And if you *do* find somethin, I have a perfectly good explanation for it or else you made it up and forgot to put somebody at the back door."

Four days later, Leon "Sniffles" Sturgeon, ace investigative reporter for *The Miami Herald,* shows up at my trailer house wipin his nose with his sleeve, and he says, "Mr. Briggs, we have evidence that you never have sex. Anywhere. Anytime. With anybody. And we feel like the public has a right to know this. It says something about your character."

And then he handed me the following transcript:

May 15, 2:25 p.m.: Subject Briggs departs Lake Grapevine Recreational Vehicle Park and Mini-Warehouses, drives 1974 metallic blue Toronado with missing fenders to Bobo's Package Liquors, purchases two cases Corona, one case Pearl, two six-packs Old Milwaukee. Drives to Le Bodine Personal Grooming Salon and Aerobic Dancewear, a portable building on Grapevine Highway, enters, departs twenty minutes later accompanied by Brenda "Biscuit-face" Washington, a part-time stylist and full-time shampoo girl. Background reveals said "Biscuit-face" to be addicted to Old Milwaukee tall boys.

May 15, 4:30 p.m.: Subject re-enters trailer house, accompanied by alleged female escort. Ten minutes later, said "Biscuit-face" emerges in hurried manner, heard to remark "I told you to get tall boys, and now I come all the way over here for *nothin.*" Female hitchhikes approximately one-half mile before being picked up by Lute Fenwick, wealthy Western Auto dealer from Cleburne, Texas.

May 15, 6:45 p.m.: Subject re-emerges, clutching partially empty Corona bottle, scratching stomach. Subject drives to Don Carter's All-Star Lanes in Fort Worth, strikes up conversation with Babbs "Babette" Babson, driver of the Don Carter's All-Star Lanes cocktail-service golf cart. Subject places hand on black stocking worn beneath subject Babson's orange hot pants and whispers something inaudible that includes the word "aardvarking."

May 15, 7:52 p.m.: The Fort Worth Fire Department successfully disengages subject's upper torso from the automatic pin-setting device in lane 37.

May 15, 8:57 p.m.: Subject drives to Debonair Dance Land in Dallas, walks onto dance floor, and announces he is going to "work my way through the alphabet—anybody named Abby here?" Subject is evicted by two husky gay mud-wrestlers wearing see-through football jerseys. Subject passes out under a '57 Chrysler after reciting all of the dueling statutes in the Texas Constitution.

May 16, 5:15 a.m.: Subject returns to trailer park, clutching a see-through football jersey.

And it goes on and on, going into the most intimate details of my personal life, and all I got to say is:

1. It's all lies.

2. I didn't know he was a gay guy.

My only point was: we all went crazy at the same time.

I've Heard of Kinky, but This Is Ridiculous

But some of us went a *lot* crazier than others. The nineties got so kinky that some men went totally off the deep end and became even more nutzoid than preachers and politicians.

For example, the California Bar Association is considering a controversial new rule that would "forbid lawyers to demand sex as a condition of representing a client." What's interesting to me about this particular battle is . . .

1. How many lawyers have been trading litigation for fornication? Wouldn't it have to be *hordes* of attorneys doing this before you ended up with an actual bar association *rule* about it? I wish we'd known about this in Texas, because three-fourths of our lawyers would have been working trade-outs for *years* by now, and we could have held down legal costs to no more than two, three hundred an hour.

2. If it's "controversial," what are the lawyers who are *opposed* to the rule saying?

"We only trade sex for services in the case of indigent people who, let's face it, would have to give us the shirts off their backs if forced to pay full price. So, instead, we let them get *on* their backs, and we get *under* their shirts. It's a humanitarian thing."

Or "Why should it be illegal to have a few drinks with a client, maybe take in a porno movie, maybe get a room later, and then prepare for the case by testifying our brains out? I mean, it happens all the time."

3. What kind of client would *want* sex with his or her lawyer? After all, if his price is *your* body, then think of what happens when he gets into the courtroom and another *lawyer* offers him something. As any cop will tell you, amateurs should *never* try to compete with professional prostitutes. It's a good way to get killed.

4. Does the lawyer have to report the actual fair-market value of the sex on his income taxes? Can you imagine the arguments with the CPA?

The lawyer says, "Five hundred bucks? No way! She was ugly! She was *fifty bucks* if anything!"

And the CPA says, "But if she was fifty bucks, then, based on the time you spent on her case, you've reduced your hourly rates to four dollars. You slept with her twice—right?—and then you did twenty-five hours worth of legal work. The IRS is just not gonna buy it."

"Okay, maybe she was worth a hundred, but only because she gave me a ride home."

5. The feminists say that this is a men-preying-on-women issue. If I were a woman (you scoff?) I'd be royally hacked off about somebody saying this is a female issue. This is a *stupidity* issue.

162

IRON JOE BOB

An El Lay assemblywoman with the great name of Lucille Roybal-Allard has a solution: Any lawyer "considering entering into a sexual relationship with a client" should explain all the "potential pitfalls" and suggest the client go to a second lawyer and get consultation on whether to enter into the sexual relationship and then sign a "written waiver" saying it's okay to be doing lawsuits and sex at the same time with the same person.

Whew! And we thought prenuptials were a mess.

"Hey, babe, let's blow this joint. But, before we do, could we run by the all-night legal clinic and fill out a few papers. Nothing heavy. Don't worry about it. Maybe you haven't been hanging around the singles bars much. Yeah, *all* the lawyers do it now. It's a form of courtship."

Actually, I can think of a great reason *not* to pass this rule.

If you sleep with the lawyer, then there's one thing you never have to worry about. He *has to call you back!*

I think you ladies should reconsider.

Okay, so that's already about a ninety-seven on the Sexual Craziness Scale, but what you may not realize is that lawyers who sleep with their clients, judges who harass their clerks, bosses who hit on their secretaries are now, in the age of feminism, actually *proud* of themselves—because it makes the woman even *more of a challenge.*

Getting dizzy yet?

In a country always in search of new status symbols, mere material possessions are no longer enough. Mercedes? Sorry, you're ten years too late. Ferrari? Okay, five years. Cellular phone? The *maid* has a cellular phone. Designer shirts? Entire *gangs* in the South Bronx wear shirts with "Ralph Lauren" on the front.

No, we've reached the end of this particular Go-Kart ride. If you wanna be hip now, it's got to be something you can't just *buy.* It's gotta be something you *do.*

Here, in ascending order of importance, are the status symbols of the nineties:

1. Sexually harass someone in your office. Sure, you'll take a little heat at first. Sure, your superior will call you in and give you the lecture on "inappropriate behavior." Sure, the gal (or guy) will think you're scum. But, *after* you've been put through the ringer, women will come out of the woodwork to tell you how badly you were treated and how everyone else is overreacting. You'll become notorious, then sympathetic, then popular, and eventually—after the story has made it through several rounds of office gossip—*legendary.*

2. Show up at a party with somebody who once made a porno movie. In 1972, this would get you fired. In 1992, your boss will come over the next day and say, "Soooo, is she *really* like that? I mean, does she make those noises?" Because make no mistake about it—*everybody* in this world has a VCR. If they didn't see her *before* you showed up with her, they've seen her now.

3. Marry somebody thirty years younger than you. This is something you can do that ticks off *almost everybody* except the person you're marrying, and it has one added advantage. They all have to *pretend* that they're happy for you.

4. Have an affair with someone who promises you she'll pose for *Playboy* later and tell everyone exactly what you did to her. To do this, you've got to be at least semifamous to begin with, like a congressman or an actor or the head of a corporation. But remember—*you* get to pick the woman, because she's not gonna become famous, and *Playboy*'s not gonna be interested, until she has sex with *you.* Get it? Mucho prestige here.

5. Write a book about everyone you've ever slept with. This has one drawback. If nobody buys the book, it could be *very* humiliating. So hire a "sexual publicist" who will call up reporters who are too lazy to read the book and tell them about the juicy parts.

6. Deny everything that was said about you in someone else's book. Use the press conference to tell embarrassing sexual details about *other* people you've been with.

7. Make a movie about yourself, where it's obvious that you're a sex-craving wild animal searching for the right person. Refer to *Truth or Dare* here if you don't know what I mean.

8. Go on *Oprah* to talk about how you were in a swingers club where you had twelve different partners a night, but you realized how empty that life is, and so now you're searching for an "ordinary girl" you can settle down with. Go home and watch that phone light up.

9. Show up at the Academy Awards ceremonies with any woman *except* Kathy Bates. Act like you don't notice the designer dress that your actress escort is falling out of.

10. Start lunching with Warren Beatty.

I'm telling you, the sicker you can make it, the more popular you'll become. Give it a shot.

And speaking of sick, we also have the ultimate kinky guy for the nineties—William Kennedy Smith. Let this guy be a lesson to us all. He figured it out first. *He* knows that men went crazy in 1984 and started aardvarking around like hyenas on Methedrine, but he *also* knows that the women had a six-year head start.

So listen up, guys. If you ever get accused of date rape, sexual harassment, hanky-panky, happy fingers, or grabbing anything protected by a foundation garment—if you know what I mean and I'm sure that you do—then here's the foolproof way to get out of it.

She's a fruitcake.

Loon City.

Sure, she looks normal *now.* Sure, with her legs crossed and her makeup on and her hairdo done up like Anne Murray, *sure* she looks sane. She *wants* you to think she's sane.

But, Your Honor, I ask you, is this normal behavior? When I went to pick her up, she came to the door holding an eighteen-inch turkey-basting fork in her hand. She kept calling it "Shirley" and licking gizzard juice off of it. Then, on the way to the movie, she kept popping her eyeballs out of their sockets and saying "I bet you can't do this."

I know I know I know, you're wondering, "Well, why didn't you do something?" But you don't understand. *Now,* in retrospect, I wish I *had* done something. But, at the time, I just thought she was from New Jersey or something.

I took her to see *Cape Fear.* Halfway through the movie, she said, "Robert De Niro is trying to kill my baby."

Naturally, I said, "What baby?"

And she said, "It's a secret."

And that's all she would say. "It's a secret." So we have a fork-wielding eyeball-popping woman here having delusions about Robert De Niro doing some kind of weird abortion on her.

I would like to add right here, Your Honor, that I mean no disrespect to Miss [deleted by CNN] when I say she said these things. She may have had a perfectly good reason for carrying a turkey fork around and putting smushed strawberries in the soles of her shoes. Oh, I didn't mention that?

Yes. Yes. Absolutely. Strawberries in both shoes. I didn't ask about it at the time, because I thought it would be impolite.

Okay, where was I?

Next I asked her if she'd like to come see my house. I figured, "What the hell, she's crazy but she has a nice set of . . . " Let me stop myself right here. Your Honor, I realize that what I'm about to tell you is a very immature and shallow thing. It's very difficult for me to talk about. I'm not proud of myself.

Anyway, when we got inside she asked me to make a noise like Pee-Wee Herman and show her my Blockbuster Video membership card.

No sir. No, I have no idea why she asked for that. I had my hands down her dress at the time, but she was getting excited, and so I pulled out the Blockbuster card and showed it to her. She calmed down after that.

Well, then, she asked me if . . . this is hard for me . . . she asked me if I would be willing to make love to her while she was running across a lawn screaming.

Again, in retrospect, I guess I should have known something was wrong. But you have to remember—*I thought she was from New Jersey!*

So I did it. Just to make her happy. I didn't even enjoy it.

After we were finished, she said, "I would like to have sex with Elmer Fudd."

And I laughed.

It was the laugh that set her off. She became very upset. She started screaming. And she claimed that I raped her. Her precise words were, "I popped my eyeballs for you, and then you raped me."

No sir, I really don't know what she meant.

I wish I did, Your Honor. My attorneys used the term "erotomania" . . .

Oh, yes, okay, Your Honor, I guess that *would* be hearsay and speculation. I won't say "erotomania" again. No sir, I won't.

I wish we had witnesses, Your Honor. I know it sounds very strange. Thank you for listening.

You guys understand now?

Use this.

I don't know *why* it works, but it works.

Dating Is So EIGHTIES

To show you how pitiful most men are in the nineties, I think we need to look no further than phone sex. And so here, once and for all, I would like to state my position on phone-sex advertising, phone-sex employees, and, to be brief, phone sex itself.

First of all, I find it perfectly acceptable in a free and open society if people want to have sex with their phones, as long as they do it in the privacy of their own home or at least in the privacy of a phone booth. But *not* one of those phone booths that doesn't have any doors on it, because 1) it might offend older people who think phone sex is "kinky," 2) it's highly unsanitary to have sex with a public phone, even if the phone is equipped with a condom, and 3) the receiver is up so high off the ground that you could hurt yourself.

Next, I'd like to say hi to Wicked Draculina of Manti, Utah, who I met on the Salt Lake City Party Line one night when I was in town making a speech to the Southwestern Utah Beef Producers. *I called back! I really did!* There must have been something wrong with that number you gave me. The guy who answered was really weird. All he ever said was "Bueno K.S." I don't know anybody named Bueno K.S.

But, most important, I'd like to point out the service that phone-sex lines provide to the American culture and economy. If it weren't for phone-sex lines, independent TV stations that show *The Lone Ranger* all night would have *no income at all.* You can't expect these station owners to get every John Davidson info-mercial for hair-care products that comes along. They've got to make a living.

But the main function of phone-sex lines is that they provide employment for fat girls. I love fat girls. And if you've ever known anybody who works on a phone sex line, then you know it's true . . . it's an employment agency for Holsteins in Spandex tights.

Think about it for a minute. What do the ads offer?

Conversations with women who are *starved* for sex.

What else do they offer?

Conversations with women who are starved for sex *with you.* No matter *what* you look like or how many cars are rusting in your front yard.

What kind of woman can do this job?

Well, actually, *any* woman can do this job.

What kind of woman can do this job *well?*

Fat girls. Some of em can talk about sex for *hours.* Some of em, with exceptionally vivid imaginations, get so excited that the first minute costs forty bucks, and each additional minute is only twenty-four cents. And you know why?

Cause that first minute is an experience you'll never forget. These are sex-starved office buildings in dresses. When they say "Hello, I'm glad you called," they are *glad you called!*

You see the beauty of this? The guy's happy. The gal's happy. Three members of my world-famous chorus line, the

Dancing Bovina Sisters (eight girls weighing a total of one ton), were phone-sex operators before they became stars. And you know why they were so good at it? One of em told me.

"Most women," she said, "use sex to try to get something from a man. But we're *fat*. We know how to use a man to *get sex.*"

You see the difference? It's subtle, I realize, but it's what made phone sex what it is today.

Now the reason I bring up phone sex, though, is that I want you to realize there are actually guys *going bankrupt* from this stuff. *That* is how pathetic the American male has become.

In fact, even as I write this, we're in that time of the year that's *extremely* dangerous for lonely guys, the time right after it turns spring when all your hormones start doing the Watusi but every time you approach a woman they act like they suddenly have to wash their hair, do their laundry, and clean their furnace.

You consider a blind date.

Don't do it! Never forget *why* they're "blind" in the first place—because *only* a blind man would date em *after* he saw em.

You drink eight Old Milwaukee tall boys and start considering a 900 number.

Don't do it! Never forget *why* they're called 900 numbers—because you can't make a phone call without spending at least 900 bucks.

You consider a singles bar.

Don't do it! Never forget the kind of guys who go to singles bars—guys like *you!* And never forget the kind of *gals* who go to singles bars—gals who *don't mind* being bird-dogged all night by ninety-seven guys *exactly like you.*

You have experiences in those places that can depress you for months.

You consider a hooker.

There you go. Now you're *talking.* It's safe. It's a lot less pathetic than 900 numbers. Sometimes the women have actual personalities. And, unlike every other kind of male-female relationship, you always know the *total price* up front.

That's why I wanna make sure you guys that are feeling like three-legged toad frogs this year, and are likely to get into some kind of hooker-client relationship that tomorrow morning you'll act like you didn't get into because in your mind you've convinced yourself that you didn't do it even though we all know you did, including you—I want all you guys to clip out this chapter and carry it in your wallet everywhere. Because the following are the ten rules you can *never forget* when dealing with a lady of the Professionalis Aardvarkus persuasion.

1. When you say "How much?" the answer should never be "How much do you want to spend?"

2. When you say "How much?" and she gives you prices for more than fifteen different varieties of recreation, and you don't recognize at least half of them, politely ask to be excused. You could *die* here.

3. No matter what happens, never apologize. Act like that's what you *meant* to do.

4. Never call her a hooker. She'll think you mean she *looks* or *acts* like a hooker. And every woman who looks and acts like a hooker, *even the ones who are hookers,* do *not* consider themselves hookers. It's a female thing. Trust me.

5. When she says "Are you a cop?" imagine you're going through the metal detector at the airport. Jokes will only get you in trouble.

6. If you *are* a cop, tell the truth. She'll never believe you.

7. More than 74,000 times a year, lonely pathetic guys like us pay additional money *after* we're finished. It's that guilt

thing. Hookers know this. You know it's coming when they say "Don't you have *anything* else?" If you fall for this, don't tell anybody.

8. Ask her if she's a cop.

9. If she comes to your house, when you open the door, say "Susan, it's so good to see you—is your mom all right?" This is because *everybody* is watching her. All the people you *think* are watching, *are* watching—and if you don't say this, everyone will know how pitiful you are.

10. After it's over, when you *realize* how pitiful you are, console yourself with the knowledge that men have been doing this for *millions* of years. Hookers know this, too.

What the Hell, Let's Get Married

L et's think about our fable once more. (You thought I forgot, didn't you? The reason it seems that way is there's a *whole* lot of stuff to say about how the Dark Princess hacks off your head.) So there the young brave is, standing in the forest, headless, wondering what the hell he does now.

> *And a tall skinny man appeared, carrying a long stick and smoking a Marlboro. And he looked at the young brave and said, "Your goddamn head is lying on the ground. You must have met Shirley." And the young brave didn't answer, because he had no head. And the tall skinny man walked over to the head, picked it up, and said, "Okay, I'm only gonna do this one time." And he screwed the young brave's head on straight.*
>
> *That man was called Iron Joe Bob.*

Sooner or later, sometime in your life, you're gonna need to find your own Iron Joe Bob. You're gonna have to reach into that deep innermost part of yourself that says, "That bimbo just ripped your head off." And you're gonna look around, and you're gonna say, "Screw this."

Women are not the answer. Dating is not the answer. Hookers are not the answer. You look around and you see people who never wake up at 8 a.m. asking questions like "Is this my car?" and "How long have you had that hickey on your chin?" You wonder who these people are and how you can become one of them.

They're called "married people."

And so you ask somebody to marry you. And you're *amazed* that you never thought of this before, because have you ever noticed in the fairy tales that, as soon as there's a marriage, the story is over? Ever wonder why that is? Ever wonder why the princess never says "No, I won't marry you"? Ever wonder why the prince doesn't just forget all the dragon part of the story—the part where you puke on the floor at Studio 54—and go right to the "Let's get married" part?

Because *nobody ever explained it to us.*

All right, I'm gonna explain it to you.

All of a sudden, just in the last two, three years, marriage has become hip again. In fact, if you want publicity these days, you've got to come out in favor of eternal marriage with your one true love.

Have you noticed this?

Have you noticed how all the gossip magazines and the tabloids and *People* magazine and *Us* magazine and *Self* magazine and *We* magazine and *Them* magazine and *Hey Y'all* magazine all agree on this?

Every Valentine's Day they do articles on which celebrity couples are making *"real* commitments." Are Richard Gere and Cindy Crawford serious? How could they be? He hasn't bought her a ring. What about Demi Moore and Bruce Willis? They've had one kid, with another on the way—*fifty points!*

One writer even went so far as to say the couple with the

"best prospects for remaining married" is Prince Charles and Lady Di. Even though he's never at home, and prefers to see his old girlfriends, he would *never* get a divorce, and so that celebrity marriage gets a perfect score. They may or may not like each other. They may or may not want to *be* with each other. They may or may not hope their spouse is squashed by a piece of earth-moving equipment. But, by God, they're *married.*

Wasn't it less than ten years ago when the same magazines were glamorizing the *un*married? Joe Namath was a huge celebrity for years—every new girlfriend on his arm was a photo opportunity—until the day he got married, and then he vanished from the tabloids. In other words, *true* monogamy was boring copy. Who ever wrote about Jimmy Stewart's wife? They'd been married since before the beginning of time.

But now, sometime in the last couple of years, all the rules have changed. Champions of the gossip magazines are people like Paul Newman and Joanne Woodward, a thirty-year couple, or Hume Cronyn and Jessica Tandy, who were married in 1634.

Even more surprising, I think everyone has finally become bored with Warren Beatty. With each passing year, the press feels more freedom to take wild potshots at the guy, implying that he's *using* whoever he happens to be dating, when this is probably not the case at all. The truth is, the older he gets, the more likely he's not the user, but the usee. And now, after all, even *he* decided to get married. But he had no choice. The times demand it.

Or how about the way they talk about Barbara Bush and her Significant Other? They speak of George and Barbara's "deep respect" for each other. They mention how much they "still like each other's company." They talk about how George "has always trusted her opinion."

They don't exactly paint a picture of two people who do a lot of Japanese massage in the hot tub.

The implication is that the most successful marriages are like high school band trips that last forever, or maybe like your dad's birthday party. You already know what's gonna happen. You know what he's gonna say. He knows what presents he's gonna get. But it makes you happy to *go through the motions.*

The other implication is that marriage is an endurance test. All the magazines give out points for sheer longevity. Ten years together—they *must* be in love. Split up after six months—they *must* be losers, afraid to commit, selfish.

Actually, I think a better argument could be made for the other way around. Marriage is unnatural. If two people have been together ten years and "they've never had a serious argument" (always said with pride), then what usually happens? They finally have one big *doozie* of an argument, and all their friends just *hope* there are no handguns in the house. If two people are profiled on *Lifestyles of the Rich and Famous* as having a "dream family" and a "love that never grows old," what *always* happens? Divorce within two years.

See, you should *never* tempt God on this stuff. *He* knows it's unnatural.

And the people that split up after six months—many of whom are actors—tend to be expressive, emotional people who say *exactly what they mean* from day one, instead of waiting fifteen years.

The ones who wait fifteen years say things like:

"I always thought he would change."

"I gave him the best years of my life."

Who needs this kind of whining?

"He was a jerk, so I walked."

Healthy. American. The Rambo Code of Love.

Or, perhaps more realistic:

"The first two years we were married, we beat each other with lead pipes, but since then we've learned to be more accepting."

That I believe.

That is an American marriage.

Or:

"I decided I didn't want to see my husband for three weeks, so I went to Miami by myself."

This is a woman who loves the guy.

In other words, the only thing longevity really buys you is one less time you have to hunt for a new apartment.

Wouldn't it be nice if somebody, one time, at some magazine, somewhere in this universe, just said, "Johnny Depp and Winona Ryder are engaged to be married. Let's all hope they're happy. Of course, only *they* know whether they're happy or not. It's the kind of thing that's inside *them,* not *us.* It's something we *can't* know. So, until they say otherwise, let's assume they *are.*"

Wouldn't that be nice?

Fat chance.

Sorry I got off on that. Here's my point. You're probly wondering why Iron Joe Bob doesn't show up until the point of marriage. Simple. That's when the whole process starts. You've always *been* a weenie, but up until now you probly didn't *know* you were a weenie. It takes an actual wife to point these things out.

If you *don't* have an Iron Joe Bob in your life, it takes at least three wives to find out all the things that Iron Joe Bob can tell you in five minutes.

I have this one ex-wife . . . naw, excuse me, she's not an ex-wife, she's the *anti-wife.* The anti-wife used to show up in my nightmares, with purple four-inch Lee Press-on Nails, screaming at me to pick up her sister at the airport. Sometimes the anti-wife had snakes growing out of her hair. But usually the anti-wife said just one sentence:

"I will not have that *thing* in my house."

It didn't matter what the thing was—a baseball bat, a Weed-Eater, a '69 Hemi Cuda engine, the July issue of *Melons Monthly*—

whatever it was, the anti-wife would point at it like it was three quarts of German shepherd puppy doo. And I would say to myself, "I could *swear* she never looked like that when I first met her." What happened? Did she go to the Neiman-Marcus beauty spa and turn in her fake arms and legs and eyebrows and get her *real* ones back? I'm talking about physical stuff—as if I married a bionic wife, but the bionic wife was just a temporary model. When the batteries run down, it becomes . . .

The anti-wife!

I've even got pictures to prove it. Here's the wife, 1984, looking like the checkout girl at Eckerd's drugstore. She smiles at strangers. Her eyes sit back in her face where they belong. Her legs have curves in them. And then here's the wife in 1988, when she's become the anti-wife. We're talking bug-eyed lizard lady, with more bulges than a fat man's lawn chair.

Then there's the money thing.

1984: "I don't really care about money. You handle it."

1988: *"You owe me!"*

Every time the anti-wife shows up, I feel like Paul Newman in *The Hustler* when he has to face George C. Scott at the end.

"You owe me MONEY!"

The anti-wife is certain that you're hiding her money, or making more money than she knows about, or *secretly* working a night shift at K-mart to cheat her out of eighty bucks a week.

And then the most amazing thing happens. The anti-wife changes back. She *mutates.* You run into her in the mall, and there she is again, 1984 model—arms, legs, eyebrows, everything in the right place. She even smiles at you. She's gone bionic again.

I'm telling you guys this for your own good. Don't fall for it. The parts can be traded in. Within two months of your marrying her, you know what you're gonna hear:

"I will not have that *thing* in my house."

That's the kind of thing Iron Joe Bob can tell you up front.

Get a Job

There's a certain time between the Marriage and the Anti-Wife called "Hauling Your Ashes." (This is not to be confused with "Getting Your Ashes Hauled," which is dealt with in my previous book, *Nine Ways from Sunday.*) Some men hate this part, because it means getting up in the morning and actually putting on "clothing." You don't think about this when you get married. You think it'll be one long Club Med Coco Loco. But then reality sets in: you need funds. More important, your new wife has had too many Coco Locos and you need *out of the house.*

But nobody wants to just make money. The modern man, in the nineties, must have a *career.* And to have a career, you must do something hip. And to do something hip, you normally need something called "education." But this is far too time-consuming. So you do something that *looks* creative, but in reality any idiot can do it. You make movies.

In the fifties, college students wanted to write the Great American Novel.

This won't work in the nineties, because college students

can't read. So now they want to make the Great American Movie.

Film school is *very* hip. If you're rich and smart and connected, you go to USC Film School. If you're not quite as hip, you go to New York University Film School. If you have to claw your way to the top, you go to UCLA Film School. But even if you have no money and you're dumber than dirt, you at *least* go to the University of Arkansas at Pine Bluff Film School, because film is something you can get your heart and soul into. The great thing about film is that, actually, *nobody* knows *exactly* how they're made—which means that maybe even *you* can make one.

And, if you're very lucky and very talented, you'll have a career that goes like this:

Freshman year: You watch every film that Akira Kurosawa ever made, in the original Japanese, *without subtitles,* because you believe film "is an art form that's only limited by words. The film is my canvas, not my soapbox. Kurosawa showed us how to paint, not to preach."

Sophomore year: You go to movies from France where nothing happens but "the cinematography is exquisite." You talk to your friends about "the nature of light as the essence of life."

Junior year: You have heated discussions about whether the films of John Ford are "parables of the violent American soul" or "damn good Westerns."

Senior year: You make your first film. It's called *Chicago Interlude,* the story of a housewife-turned-prostitute who is driven to suicide by her shame.

Now you're twenty-two years old. You go to Hollywood. You have meetings. You show everyone your film. Guys named Murray watch it and tell you how great it is. Finally, one of them offers you a job—to direct *Naked Cannibal Women.* You have three weeks to get the script ready, four weeks to make the movie, and you'll get $5,000 when you turn it in.

And what do you say? Do you say, "Well, it's not the kind of

Kurosawa visionary piece I was looking for?" *Of course not!* You say, "All right, I'll direct *Naked Cannibal Women,* but in my hands this movie will become a *statement.* Through the experience of the naked cannibal women, we will see a powerful parable for the feminist struggle against male . . . uh . . . male *dietary practices."*

And so you go out and make *Naked Cannibal Women,* and when it's finished, a producer calls you in and says, "Okay, what's your background?" And you say, "Well, uh, I made this one little exploitation picture, but I'm ready to move *beyond* that now." And the producer says, "How much did the picture cost?" And you tell him how much it cost. And then the producer says, "I need somebody to make *Viking Lust Queens."*

And do you say "No, I'm really beyond that now"? *Of course not!*

You say, "I always bring my pictures in under budget."

And so ten years later, you've not only got *Viking Lust Queens* on your credits, but you've also made *Blood Pact, Lust Devils, The Secretary, Blood Pact II, Mad Mama,* and *Skull.*

Now you're saying things like, "Twenty years from now, people will realize that these are the true statements about our culture. Angie Dickinson and Robert Culp are both interested in *Skull 2.* That shows you how far this type of genre experiment has come in terms of star acceptance."

And then finally, when you're forty years old, you get your big break—a two-part movie-of-the-week starring Johnny Depp, Traci Lords, Glenn Ford, and Denzel Washington, with "a special appearance by David Carradine as Booger Johnson." The project is called *Don't Let Mommy Beat Me Anymore,* and it airs on Monday and Tuesday of sweeps week, scoring a solid 21 Nielsen rating the first night, dipping to an 18 the second night. The show is nominated for two Emmys and receives a special citation from the President's Council on Child Abuse.

Ten years later, you've made twenty-five more TV movies,

specials, and dramatic pilots, including *Confessions of a Crackhead,* starring Wayne Newton.

"Television is the true American art form," you are saying now. "We can all be proud of this work. We've changed things with these projects."

And then one day you're fifty-five, and you're thinking, "You know, after all these years, maybe I could just direct one movie with Robert De Niro, or maybe one of those fantasy things, or a special-effects picture." And you take a few meetings. And everybody is very polite to you.

And then a guy named Murray says to you one day, "Have you seen this tape? Lemme show it to you. Kid out of NYU Film School made it. It's called *Akron Interlude.* There's a great part at the end where the woman commits suicide. I'm thinking of giving the kid a shot."

And you know it's over. You know something got lost in there, but you don't know exactly what it is. You know you never really did anything wrong, but you know that *something* got between you and your intentions.

Something did.

It's called money.

That's why you need Iron Joe Bob in your life—to figure these things out in advance, to keep your head screwed on straight. And always remember this:

A *woman* cannot take the place of Iron Joe Bob. This is the mistake we all make. We think a female can do a male's job. No way, José. You know what a woman would say to a guy who's fifty-five and never did what he wanted to do?

"Oh well, that's all past now. We're happy, aren't we?"

They *never understand this work stuff.* Don't even try.

All right. The first thing you need when you enter the job market is a great résumé. Education is helpful, but it's not *nearly* as important as the résumé.

You've probly heard me talking about my cousin Cletis Coverdale, who lives in Waxahachie, Texas, but never has been able to find a job for the last twelve years and so he's gonna take a crack at the Superconducting Supercollider that's supposed to create seventeen million jobs in a giant tunnel under Waxahachie. Cletis came by last week, cause he heard I knew how to type and he needed to "update" his résumé.

So I asked him what kind of job he was looking for.

"Hunnerd a week and get off weekends."

See, once you've got yourself a clearly defined goal like that, then you're well on the way to being an employed individual. So up at the top of Cletis's résumé, I put "Career Objective: Detail-oriented self-starter with bottom-line savvy seeks entry-level trainee position in stable firm with growth potential."

Next thing, I asked Cletis what kind of education he had.

"I worked on my brother's truck."

I typed "Heavy equipment technology background."

"By the way," I said, "whatever happened to that truck after you worked on it? Never did see it again."

"We had to sell it for scrap," Cletis told me.

I typed "Creative problem solver."

Cletis reminded me he had three hours' credit from 1968 when he went to the Big Rig Truck Driving School over in Shreveport, but I told him we couldn't write that down because he never did graduate. "You should never put misleading information on your résumé," I said.

Next thing, we got into Cletis's employment history. It was fine up until 1976. Cletis hauled dirt for Scrim Wilks, took inventory at the Gulf station, and unloaded Christmas trees off railroad cars for the Elks Club. But ever since then, Cletis has just been sitting around the barbershop for most of the last twelve years. So at the end of the employment history, I wrote, "Due to the depressed economy, Mr. Coverdale's position was eliminated."

Under "Personal," I typed "Divorced, Smoker, Skinny as a rail," but Cletis took exception to that. "I ain't divorced," he said. "I ain't *seen* her in seven years, but we never did put the papers through."

I got out the eraser and changed it to "Involved, sort of, No dependents, Actually you wouldn't believe it."

"All right, Cletis, now we're at the point where every great résumé has to deliver the groceries. What are your specific skills for this job?"

"What job?" Cletis said.

"Running the Superconducting Supercollider."

"I'm a people person."

"*Great!* You've gotta be a people person for this. Very good."

"I'm a take-charge self-starter."

"We already said that."

"By the way, I don't smoke."

"Right."

"I chew."

"Okay, but Cletis, what's the one skill that sort of sums up your ability to manage the world's largest atomic collider? We've gotta put that on here."

"I can type twenty words a minute with two mistakes."

"That's good, but it's not quite it."

"I can use a Dictaphone. I can't type out what's on it, but I can use it."

"Also good, but it doesn't really sum it up."

"I have management consultant experience in the field."

"Bingo!"

"I should of told you that to start with. I used to run a forklift for Rusty Cheever."

"Was the forklift made up of atomic particles?"

"I reckon. I didn't ask Rusty."

"You're in."

I typed in "Customer Service Hardware Systems Management Experience." The rest of you people out there might as well not even apply.

Now I already know what a lot of you guys are thinking. You're thinking, "I already got a job. That's my whole *problem.* That's half the reason I'm so miserable."

You know what Iron Joe Bob says to that?

You are *not* in a job. You are in a prison. You don't belong there. You gotta get your hiney out of there and get a *new* job. And lemme show you what I mean.

You noticed lately how many leeches there are out there working in the field of "personnel" or "employee relations" or "work-force management" or whatever they're calling it this week?

I know these guys. And these gals. Know em real well. They're the guys who give you the little test when you show up for work the first day, the one they *claim* is a "personality profile" but is *actually* a test to show whether you're likely to embezzle half the money in the midwest division and spend it on lingerie for a mistress you're keeping in Omaha.

They're the people who give you the little cup for the drug test.

They're the people who, once a year, send you a report marked "confidential" where they evaluate your "performance" and "progress" and "attitude."

They're the ones that send you to Whiskey School in Arizona if you become a drunk.

In other words, these people are kinda like the Russian government *used* to be. They're always hanging around, watching you, judging you, evaluating you, talking to your girlfriend. It's like spending your entire life with Sally Jessy Raphael hanging around your house. "Do you think that's really in your best interests, Mr. Briggs?" "Do you think that's a mature decision, Mr. Briggs?" "Did you get a copy of the new smoking regulations, Mr. Briggs?"

And my point is, there's more and more of these people hanging around every day. They're everywhere. They're taking over entire companies. They're *forcing* people to come in for meetings about "sexual harassment sensitivity." They're like tarantulas out there, brushing their furry spindly little legs across everything and making you feel icky.

So why do people put up with it?

I'll tell you why. People put up with it because the greatest fear of the twentieth century is not that we'll all get blown up by an atomic bomb. And it's not that we'll all die of AIDS. And it's not that some guy with a bad beard will drive by in a Camaro and shoot you.

The greatest fear of the twentieth century is that you'll lose your job.

People used to quit jobs or get fired all the time, and you know what they'd do? *Go on to the next job.*

Not today. Today it's like this major trauma that requires *nine years* of therapy. Just *thinking* about losing your job gives people the shakes.

And so these people, these tarantula people, these nerdy little furry prying weirdos, just flat take over your life.

There's a solution to this. It works when you say the following words:

"I quit."

Whenever somebody starts complaining to me about what a prison their job is, I always say "So why don't you tell em to stick the job in a Sani-Can?"

And the answer is always, "Oh no, I couldn't do that. I've got a *family,* and it's really bad times right now in my industry, and jobs are scarce, and I've got a *mortgage . . . "* and blah blah blah, naming things that you *always* have. I mean, you *always* have a family, right? There's not gonna be some time in the future when you *don't* have a family. And you always have a mortgage, and you're always afraid you won't get another job. *Everybody* is afraid they won't get another job. Even people who have *never* been out of work are afraid they'll be out of work.

But you ask somebody who has quit a job, who has *really* quit a job. Somebody who didn't find a *new* job before they quit. Somebody who just said "Sayonara," and had *no idea* where they were going. Just sailed out onto the street and never looked back.

And you know what happens when you do that?

You think they feel scared, insecure, whatever?

They feel *great.*

I know ten people who have done this. They all remember it as one of the freest days of their lives.

"But, Joe Bob, that's easy for you to say, because you had somewhere else to go. That's all well and good for your actor friends and your writer friends, because they're so independent, but I don't know where my income would come from if I didn't work for Consolidated Chemical."

Nope. Nope. Nope. Nope. Nope. Listen to Iron Joe Bob on this one.

You've got it exactly backward.

Those people are independent *because* they quit their job. The independence is a *result* of it.

Do it. I highly recommend it. Let's all do it on the same day. That would have the added advantage of eliminating about 40,000 of the tarantulas, who would get blamed for not keeping the employees docile and under control.

Lemme repeat those words. It's been a lot of years since anybody's used em:

"I quit."

There are a lot worse things to lose than a job.

All right, what else do we males do to make ourselves feel better about being married?

Usually we go through this period called "investments," as in, "I think I'd like to be an independent investor." I have no idea what an independent investor is, but I know every man thinks he can be one some day.

For two years now my buddy Buster Peebles has been trying to get me to invest in llamas. I'm not making this up. Buster's got this ranch outside of Divide, Texas, that he's turned over to a herd of about fifty llamas, and he's breeding new ones all the time. If you've never seen one, they look like a giant goat that's been bred to a fat jackrabbit. They stare at you like Tony Franciosa hopped up on cocaine, and if you move too quick around em, they snap their neck straight up like a rattlesnake. It's like some animal that God didn't quite finish.

Anyhow, Buster was in town last year for the Fort Worth Fat Stock Show, where he shows his llamas and tries to win blue ribbons so he can charge some idiot $10,000 for some llama sperm. Ten years ago nobody in Texas had any llamas, but today there's twenty-seven million llamas in West Texas alone, and you know why?

"I think these llamas are gonna *take off* in the next ten years," Buster told me. "One of these female breedin llamas brought a hunnerd thousand dollars last year."

I don't know if you're acquainted with any of the Peebles, or maybe you know some llama breeders yourself, but what that means is, everybody's been talking too much about llamas down at the barbershop. "Somebody's gonna get rich off these things," they been saying, "so might as well be *us*."

(I need to take time out right here to talk to those of you who have read previous books and know that sometimes I make stuff up. I swear to God, ranchers all over Texas are walking around with beer guts hanging out over their belts, prancing proudly forward, clicking their tongues, and yanking on a leash attached to an alpaca sweater with legs.)

So I went over to Fort Worth with Buster to watch last year's Llama Exposition. See, the problem with the llama market at this particular point in time is that people keep walking up to Buster and the other llama breeders and saying, "So what do you use them things for?"

And Buster says "Pack animal."

And they just kinda nod and chew a little bit.

"State parks department uses llama pack trains to go up in the desert mountains."

"Uh-huh," they say.

"And, course, they make great pets for the kids."

And then they nod and chew some more.

So what's needed is a llama competition to show people just *exactly* what the highly trained llama can do. And so that's what they did. The llamas had to go through a ten-step obstacle course, including walking over a log, ducking under a steel rod, walking across a piece of plastic, and climbing into a horse trailer. It was truly awe-inspiring. Buster's prize llama is named Oprah Winfrey, and Oprah was a little persnickety when it came to the grueling back-up-through-a-gate competition. So Buster only got fourth place this year.

"Buster," I said, after it was all over, "tell me again what you're gonna use these llamas for. It's a pet, right?"

"This ain't a pet," Buster said. "This llama's an *investment*."

"Yall are all just gonna sell these llamas to one another, aren't you? You're just gonna trade em back and forth."

"Luanne and me are gonna *retire* on the money we make from these llamas. Joe Bob, do you realize this is one of the oldest pack animals in the world? Royalty used to have em."

"Buster, people got *pick-ups* now! People don't need pack animals!"

"That's the kind of negative thinking that'll keep you from ever amounting to anything in life."

"Buster, I think I'd rather own a hunnerd-thousand-dollar pickup than a hunnerd-thousand-dollar llama. If the llama dies, you can't sell it for parts."

I guess that was about the moment when Buster cleaned my clock. We were pretty good friends, too. See, what happened is I had challenged Buster's manhood, by implying he didn't know how to *invest.* Investment is a very male thing.

Then, next thing I know, Buster comes back to town a year later, still trying to sell his first llama, but now he's begging me to go with him over to the state fairgrounds to look at some "ostrich opportunities." Have you heard about this? It's the *latest* thing for guys like Buster to start selling back and forth to one another. So we went to the ostrich show to see why, after all these years of ranching, Buster still didn't have any three-hundred-pound birds with legs like baseball bats walking around on his ranch.

"Buster," I told him, "I'm not spending one dime on any ostrich ranching."

And he said, "That's what's wrong with you, Joe Bob. All you care about is boring, traditional animals like cows, sheep, goats. I guess you want us to just keep buying more cows, sheep, and goats. I guess that's *your* idea of a progressive, modern ranch."

And I told him, "Oh, I see your point, Buster, those animals have only been making money for about six, seven thousand years. You're right. They're gonna go out of style any day now."

So Buster just snorted at me and led me over to the special State Fair Ostrich Display where there was a "mating trio," three birds that looked like roosters that were sprayed with Agent Orange and stuffed in a giant vat of Orville Redenbacher's microwave popcorn until their necks shot up out of their bodies like squishy Q-tips.

"Very handsome animals, Buster, but I've never heard of a mating trio."

"They're kinky little rascals," said Buster.

I was afraid he'd explain, so I changed the subject. And about then, the owner of the prize ostriches, Lou Feinstein of Sallisaw, Oklahoma, walked up. Lou is the only Jewish farmer in his part of Oklahoma. Actually, he gave up most of his farm to become an ostrich broker.

"It's the wave of the future," said Lou as we stood there staring at their fat shiny necks. "It's the largest bird in the world. I clocked one of these ostriches at forty-two miles per hour—faster than my pickup." And he slapped me on the back. I told him, in the future, to slap Buster Peebles on the back, because Buster's the one who would be buying ostriches.

"Wave of the future," Lou said again.

"All right," I said, "I guess I might as well go ahead and ask. What are they good for?"

"What are they good for?" Lou said. "What are they good for?" He laughed. Buster laughed, too, so I had to wait for the hysteria to die down.

"What are they good for?" I said.

"Some of the finest boots in the world," Lou said. "Ostrich skin. Ladies shoes. Belts. Luggage."

"You put three hundred and fifty pounds of feed in this bird to make a belt?"

"And, of course, the feathers. European knights wore ostrich plumes. Very fashionable in Europe."

"Okay, that sews up the European knight market. Then we've got your ostrich-skin pumps—probly sell twenty, thirty thousand of those to American Airlines stewardesses. What else?"

"You ever see one of those fancy Easter eggs like Andy Warhol used to make? Ostrich egg. Largest egg in the world."

"Oh! Wow! Okay, now you're talking. That brings in the New York art market *and* the European knights."

"But those are all just extras," said Lou. "You wanna know what we're really doing with these birds?"

Lou waited a minute. I leaned forward. Buster leaned so far forward he looked like an ostrich.

"Health food of the nineties," said Lou. "I kid you not. Ostrich meat. Twice the protein of beef, but fewer calories, fewer carbohydrates, less fat, less cholesterol. You ever hear of an ostrich getting a heart attack?"

"Never!" said Buster.

"One dressed ostrich will yield about a hundred and twenty-five pounds of red meat," said Lou.

"And let me guess," I said. "It tastes *exactly* like chicken."

"Nope," said Lou. "That's what you'd think, isn't it? No, it's more like milk-fed prime veal."

"Do you think it's too late to get in on this?" Buster said.

"Buster!" I was doing my best. "Have you paid for all those llamas yet?"

But Buster could no longer hear me.

"Too late?" said Lou. "Too late! You're my first customer today, Mr. Peebles."

"Just one more question," I said. Lou looked at me like "You screw this up and I'll feed you to an ostrich."

"And the question is, what are ostriches being sold for, right now, this year, at the Texas State Fair? Not in the future. Right now."

"Primarily," said Lou, "the ostriches produced in the United States today are sold for breeding purposes."

"I knew it! I knew it! It's just like the llamas. Yall are just trading em back and forth, one to another, aren't you?"

But by that time, Buster was whipping out his checkbook. As they walked away, arm in arm, I could hear Buster saying, "So tell me about this mating *trio* business."

And Lou said, "Mr. Peebles, what you might prefer is a mating *quartet*, or perhaps a full orchestra . . . "

So here's where you need Iron Joe Bob to tell you the truth about investments:

The only people that get rich in "investments" are the people that were already rich before they made the investments. Do you hear what I'm saying? This stuff is not for you and me. This stuff is for Lou Feinstein and Michael Milken.

All right, so what's your next option?

Politics, right?

No no no no no no no.

Have I made that clear?

Here's all you need to know about the way men behave as soon as they go into politics:

Teapot Dome.

Tammany Hall.

Iran-Contra.

Q. What do these three scandals have in common?

A. Nobody can ever remember what they're about.

The only thing they're good for, really, is to be used in SAT questions—just obscure enough to separate the college-bound men from the sniveling bambinos.

And you may be wondering: How does such a thing happen? How do we have a political scandal like Iran-Contra that lasts *seven years,* involves two presidents, uncovers actual crimes among members of the C.I.A., the military, and the State Department—and everyone's eyes glaze over when you mention it?

There may be five people in the whole world who can even tell you the whole story of Iran-Contra. One is special prosecutor Lawrence Walsh (and even he probably has to refer to notes). One is probably a reporter somewhere who's writing a book on the subject. And there are three guys who just haven't been indicted yet.

How do this many people, from this many different places, tell lies this successfully for this long?

Easy. I don't think a single one of them *believes* he's lying.

It's not politics that's changed. It's the definition, in the political world, of what exactly is a lie.

So we have the ten Iran-Contra non-lies:

1. "It wasn't my decision." This is the most popular one. The whole thing goes like this: "Yeah, I think I know what went on, but it wasn't *directly* my responsibility, and it wasn't *directly* my decision, and so I can't *really* know what was going on, and so I choose to keep my mouth shut. This is not a lie because I don't know enough to be telling a lie."

   I don't think I really have to explain this one, do I? It's really popular with second-graders.

2. "Once you let one cat out of the bag, there's no end to this stuff." This is the theory by which you withhold one or two things you know, because if you were to tell those one or two things, it would lead to a hundred other things that would jeopardize the safety of the country. Just exactly *how* it would jeopardize the safety of the country, you're not sure, but it *would.* Or at least it might.

3. "There are a lot of gray areas in these laws passed in the seventies." After the Watergate scandal, and again after the C.I.A. plot to assassinate Castro was exposed, we passed a bunch of ethics laws. The great thing about them is that there are *no* gray areas in them. They simply say, "You can't do this, and you can't do that, and if there's any doubt in your mind, then the answer is 'No way, José.' If there's *still* doubt in your mind, you have to ask a congressional committee before proceeding." These are the most *un*gray laws ever written. They're actually the *first* laws ever passed saying the C.I.A. and military can't get involved in dirty tricks. The problem is, after they were passed, the C.I.A. and the military continued to say, "Now what exactly does *this* part of the law mean? We don't understand it." Have you ever seen a really guilty burglar on the witness stand? "I'm sorry, I don't understand that question." "Could you repeat that question, please?" "Are you asking me if I did it *knowingly*, or if I did it?" And he *believes* that he's being truthful. He believes, in fact, that if you don't ask him the questions in *exactly* the right way, then he's innocent.

4. "I haven't been able to locate any evidence of that." This is the adult equivalent of "My cat ate my homework."

5. "This was *never discussed* in my presence." (Said with great self-righteousness.) Conspiracies are almost always never discussed. When the lowest of lowlifes conspire to do something, they never *directly* discuss it. Drug dealers don't even use the word "drugs."

6. "I was under oath to protect national secrets, and I believed that these were covered by that oath." To make yourself believe this, you go home every night and say to your wife, "Honey, there are things I can't tell you." That makes you

feel important and—more important—*legal.* You *wanted* to tell your wife, but you didn't. So later on, when the committee wants to know what you didn't tell your wife, how could you possibly tell *them* what you wouldn't tell your wife?

7. "I was not apprised of that operation." This means that thousands of pages of memos crossed your desk, *referring* to "that operation," but you were smart enough not to ask anybody what it was about. This is a popular lie in Russia, home of the best bureaucrats in the world, where they've learned "If you never ask, you'll never *be* asked."

8. "These congressional committees are full of politicians, trying to get votes, who have no interest in the truth." Sometimes this is at least partly true. Unfortunately for someone using this particular lie, these congressional committees also have subpoena power, oversight authority, and the legal right to find out any damn thing they wanna find out. It's the way we set it up.

9. "These media guys always make a mountain out of a molehill." Sometimes this is also true. Unfortunately, under the law, most of the "molehills" are already felonies.

10. "I don't recall." Yes, almost twenty years later, there are still a few who will use this phrase popularized by the immortal H. R. Haldeman. This time, though, we have professional liars who have *trained* themselves *not to recall.* Ever since Watergate, as soon as one of these guys gets remotely close to a crime, they shred documents in advance, they hold up their hand (reminding colleagues not to tell them *too much*), they tear up their notes, they make sure nothing is too close to their desk—so that when the time comes, they can listen patiently to the question and say, with a clear conscience, "I don't recall."

The government, you see, becomes more like the Mafia every day. So this is one career choice you do *not* wanna make. Trust me.

Then there's the guys who are simply "tycoons." They don't buy anything, they don't sell anything, they don't really do anything. Even when they put up an office building, it's paid for with somebody else's money, and whoever's money it is doesn't even *know* it's his money, because it's some pension fund held in a bank in Liechtenstein. You know these guys? Iacocca. The Trumpster. T. Boone Pickens. H. Ross "I'm a Pussycat" Perot.

I like to think that I could have written *The Art of the Deal:*

A lot of people ask me, they say, "Joe Bob, what's a typical day in your life like? I mean, what do you *do* all day?" So I thought I'd give you an idea of a typical Joe Bob Briggs business day (excerpted from my upcoming book *Briggs on Briggs: The Search for Briggs*).

6 a.m.: Whoever's in bed with me wakes up screaming.

7 a.m.: I remember there's somebody in bed with me, and I wake up screaming.

8 a.m.: After my morning hosedown, I'm ready to start the day.

9 a.m.: My first business call is to "Jocko" Vernon, a businessman in West Palm Beach, Florida. I've been working a deal with Jocko for months to purchase a USFL football team, the Dothan, Alabama, Metronomes. Jocko says we can probly close it all out by Christmas.

10 a.m.: I take a call from Sid Schoenbaum on the floor of the New York Stock Exchange. I chuckle. "Sid, you're a crazy man. Get up off the floor." I love Sid.

11 a.m.: Dan Rather calls, asking if I need any free tickets to the road show of *A Chorus Line*. It's a nice gesture from a really warm close personal friend, but I tell Dan I don't do things that way and also he's a loser.

12 noon: I call Cherry Dilday, my personal assistant, and ask her to bring me a scrambled-egg burrito from Taco Bueno. This is because important people like me think lunch is a waste of time. In fact, I think *food* is a waste of time. I call Cherry Dilday back and change my order to a Budweiser.

1:30 p.m.: The lawyers from the Beverly Hills Hotel show up to take my deposition. I hate depositions, but when you have a life as busy as mine, you have to sue people for no reason or else everbody will forget you exist. I'm currently suing the Beverly Hills Hotel for refusing to give me a room because "we have no vacancies" even though I slipped the desk clerk a couple quarters.

2 p.m.: Sid Schoenbaum calls back from the floor of the stock exchange to say there's a wild rumor that I'm attempting to take over Mattel Toys. This is the kind of thing that happens when you're famous. Actually, all I'm trying to do is acquire control of G.I. Joe and blow his head off.

3:30 p.m.: It's The Coast calling. They want me to do a New Year's Eve benefit for Calvin Klein's new perfume line, Eau de Cleveland. I tell them I can't consider it now, because I don't like getting calls from beaches in the middle of the afternoon.

6 p.m.: Yuri Dubinin, the Russian ambassador to the United Nations, stops by for a little vodka toddy. Yuri and I discuss the drive-in situation in Russia, and my plans to eventually build the first Russian drive-in outside Vladivostok. Yuri says, "We will consider. Bo Derek, yes?" I make a call and confirm a Bo Derek title for opening night.

"Nice hootniks," says Yuri.

8 p.m.: Time for a few drinks before bed. I order a case of Falstaff but nod off to sleep before I've finished the twelfth can. After all, I have to be up early in the morning to do that space-alien miniseries deal starring Valerie Bertinelli as a lost planet drifting in space. Lorimar will want to know if I've done the rewrites on the Uranus panty-raid scene. But that's tomorrow's work. All I can

think about tonight is hookers dressed up like farm animals. That's the kind of guy I am.

But you know what happens to tycoons and investment guys. They become nervous little weenies. Don't let it happen to you.

I have this friend named Larry who's as rich as a sitcom star, and so every year at this time he takes one of those European cruises where you drink champagne every night and listen to bad cabaret acts and occasionally get off the boat to look at some Madonnas or sit at a seaside café with red-checkered tablecloths where you can guzzle the local vino for thirty bucks a pop. And they have all kinds of "programs" and "seminars" and "athletic activities" on board, so you can learn how to be a real-estate agent or a professional shuffleboard coach or find out who Marcel Proust was.

Now here's the interesting part. On his daily schedule of all the "programs" and "seminars" and "cultural activities," there's always a placed marked "Free Time."

Like there's time that costs money, and then there's *free time*. But, no, that can't be what it means, because it *all* costs money on a cruise, whether you *call* it free or not.

So what they mean is, there's *prison* time and then there's *free* time.

This is when the guy's *on vacation!* This is when he's in the one place in the world where *all* the time is supposed to be free!

And after he told me about this, I started noticing this "Free Time" thing cropping up everywhere. I have a little dumplin'-face two-year-old niece who goes to Montessori School, and they have a part of the day that's "Free Time." What this means is, they can do whatever the heck they wanna do, as long as a) they don't make too much noise, b) they don't get too dirty, c) they don't steal anybody else's property, d) they don't watch the same video-tape over and over and over again, and e) they quit "Free Time" and go back to Prison Time as soon as the teacher says "Free Time" is over.

Some corporations have "Free Time" at the office. It's supposed to improve morale. It used to be called "coffee break," but now it would be better to call it Last Meal. It's the same thing they do for condemned prisoners. "Well, I guess we'll have to kill you in the morning, but let's not dwell on that. *Tonight* you can have *anything* to eat that you want. Anything at all."

Same deal. They're just saying, "Do *whatever you want.* Go wild! Have fun! Shake loose from the corporate environment. Just do it in the next fifteen minutes."

What's wrong here? When I was a kid, I'd go to these science fairs where they had "labor-saving inventions of the future," and we were all supposed to be working twenty-hour weeks by now. But what happened? We invented all these labor-saving devices, everything got faster, and we have two-thirds *less* "Free Time" than we had twenty years ago.

You know why? Because of guys like Larry who *can't stand it.* They go on vacation and they're faced with this endless stretch of "Free Time," and they start to go crazy with guilt and nervousness. There's some great Yuppie Devil God in their gut crying out, "You could have done *seventy hours* of work in the time you spent hanging around the Parthenon and chunking rocks in the Aegean. Your life is *meaningless.*"

And so they have "Free Time." They work just as much as they do when they're back home—they're getting an education, or they're becoming culturally enlightened, or they're *improving* themselves—and then, after they've done that, they can just barely face that agonizing hour of "Free Time" in the afternoon. They can suck down a couple martinis without guilt, though, because they've just read part of a book about Giotto.

They can *use* that Giotto someday. They'll be talking to that West Coast sales rep who's into European art, and they can just casually mention that magic word—"Giotto"—and pretty soon they'll be bosom buddies for life.

Or was it Giacometti? It was either Giotto or Giacometti. You start to forget these things after the second martini.

Oh no. *Two* martinis already, and the seminar on Viking anthropology is about to start. How will he possibly be able to remember the death dates of Ethelred of Aalborg? Better stop drinking and start *concentrating* on this vacation.

After all, there's more terrifying "Free Time" to face again tomorrow.

Listen to me on this one:

It's all free, you guys.

It's all free.

Now *that* is scary.

See, what's happening is we've bought into this work-your-butt-off thing so much that we're slowly going crazy and we don't even know it.

Here's a perfect example. What do the following words mean to you?

"Disgruntled postal worker."

You used to hear those words, and you'd think, "Oh, that's one of those guys with the attitude who says 'You can't buy stamps in this line! This is the express-mail line!' "

But now you hear those words—"disgruntled postal worker"—and you think, "Oh yeah, one of those guys who drives his pickup through the post office lobby, spraying AK-47 automatic weapons fire around until he's killed thirty, forty people, screaming obscenities he heard in *Taxi Driver* until the SWAT team shows up and kills him and interviews all his neighbors who say, 'I always *did* think there was something wrong with that boy—he kinda kept to hisself.' "

In other words, *what the heck is going on at the post office?*
Don't we need to figure this out?

IRON JOE BOB

I had one idea. It's that goldurn twenty-nine-cent stamp. Nobody can ever figure out how much the postage is on *anything,* and you *never* have the right change. And so you have these postal clerks standing there, day after day, week after week, waiting on fat ladies from the Sunnybrook Retirement Center who keep fumbling in their purses while they say, "Wait a minute, I just need *one more penny.* I *know* I have it. Wait. Does anyone have a penny?" And all the time the guy is sitting behind the desk, thinking, "It had to be twenty-*nine* cents. It couldn't be twenty-*five* cents, or *thirty* cents, it had to be twenty-*nine* goldang cents. And when it's *two* ounces, it's not two times twenty-nine, which would be fifty-eight, and it's not twenty-nine plus a quarter, which they could figure out, it's twenty-nine plus twenty-*four . . . "* and he's getting madder and madder and madder, and then the old lady says, "Whoops! It's two ounces! And now I have two twenty-nine-cent stamps. I would lose money if I put both of these stamps on that one letter, wouldn't I. Perhaps I need a twenty-four-cent stamp to go *with* one of the twenty-nines. Or would you suggest that I buy a fifty-three and keep both twenty-nines for later use?"

And so he can't take it anymore. He starts reading *Soldier of Fortune* magazine. His eyes bug out. He gets headaches at night. He sits up in his undershirt, watching TV, thinking, "It *never* should have been twenty-nine cents. What *idiot* would make it twenty-nine cents? Thirty cents. Thirty-five cents. That makes *sense.* But twenty-nine cents. It's a plot. It's a conspiracy. It's a conspiracy of fat ladies with shiny purses."

And pretty soon he's loading up the old Uzi, packing twenty thousand rounds of ammo into the back of his Chevy truck, and heading down to the Dead Letter Department.

It makes you think, doesn't it?

Last week I was in the post office mailing a package, and I was thinking to myself, "What should I do? Express Mail? Standard air? Plain old first class? Or parcel post, which takes about three years to get there?" And I decided, "Well, what I oughta do is choose whichever one is the cheapest."

And so I made my way up to the front of the line, and I came face-to-face with this guy who had just figured out the rates to a post office in western China for a Chinese woman who spoke no English and didn't even know how to write "China" in English on the envelope, and he took a big sigh and he looked at me with one of those pitiful expressions, like a deer on the first day of the season, as though he were saying "Now—are you gonna cause trouble, too?"

And I said, "First class, please." And gave him a *real* big smile.

I decided, let's not test it right now, you know what I mean?

See, the problem is we've got the wrong people in the top jobs in the first place—because we think "Education" is such a big deal. Every job, you get hired for your "Education." I mean, while you're *in* college, you know what bullstuff this is, because the guys getting the best education and the guys making the grades are usually two different species. But, once you get out, it doesn't matter. The D students go right in there with the A students, and everybody ponies up their "Education."

But we keep pumping weenies through the system. Here's how it works:

If you wanna go to Harvard these days, or Stanford, or Vanderbilt, or Princeton, you've got to do one of these things:

a. Make straight A's your entire life, beginning with two-year-old Montessori School.

b. Score 1590 on your SATs, and never go outside the lines of the little circles with your number two pencil.

c. Give the school $5 million.

d. Have an ancestor who went to Harvard in 1694.

e. Own office buildings in midtown Manhattan.

Or:

f. Have a fashionable skin color. (Blacks and browns are "in" this season, but yellows, whites, and whatever-that-Middle-Eastern-color-is still have to score 1590 on the SATs.)

Then, after you've passed all the standards of smarts, and wealth, and power, and skin color, you get the *privilege* of paying the school $20,000 a year, because they were gracious enough to accept you.

Who *needs* these places?

Let's take a look at who's gonna be running America in the year 2020:

a. The straight-A student. This guy's not equipped for anything except *pleasing people older than he is.* This is the whole secret to making straight A's. It has nothing to do with intelligence, or concentration, or memory, or thinking. It means you're a good con man. You've figured out the system. You've worked the system. You've conquered the system. You're like one of those Mafia guys who's worth a billion dollars but no one knows your name—because the nature of your skill is that you *hide* your ambition.

We already tried these guys. They ran the Lyndon Johnson White House. They were pitiful.

b. The guy who scores 1590 on his SATs. These people are psychopaths. They've spent seventeen thousand hours at a computer terminal by the age of twelve, and they will never have any social skills until *at least* the age of fifty-five, when they're on their fourth wife. They're the kind of people who insult everyone around them—not because they're trying to, but because they're *not paying attention.* They're so proud of their minds that they have no hearts. They're great for talking about black holes—because they *are* black holes.

We tried these guys, too. They worked at Los Alamos during the war. We're still trying to clean up after em.

c. The rich philanthropic family. This results in an actual college diploma for . . . Teddy Kennedy. I rest my case.

d. The socially prominent family. I've never understood why we fought a war two hundred years ago to get rid of royalty, get rid of class, get rid of things like social registers—and today we *worship* the British royal family, we act like the president is our *only* leader, and we keep paying deference to people on the basis of their names. The Vanderbilts, Morgans, Hearsts, Rockefellers—believe me, if it weren't for museum curators and foundation presidents constantly going after these folks' money, we'd have no use for them. One dinner party in the Hamptons creates enough boredom for a lifetime.

We tried these people. Recently. Don't bring em back.

e. The "Trumpist" (named after Donald Trump, who out-trumped himself). There are still plenty of these flashy real-estate vultures out there, buying their way into universities and endowing professorships for the study of primitive Indian tribes in Anaheim.

Nixon used these people. Ahem.

f. The professional minority. This is the newest power bloc in American higher education, a person who defines himself by his skin color, and frequently professes some "mission" to rid the universities of the privileged, the entrenched wealthy, the status quo—the *same* universities that are saying "We've got to haul some more of these People of Color in here before we get in trouble." So this person is basically a subversive—joining a club he doesn't respect, so he can take over the club, change the club, and refashion it in his own image.

We've tried these people. They run Detroit. Great job, guys.

No school that I know of admits students according to the only qualities that matter—honesty and curiosity. Give me an illiterate pig farmer with those two qualities and I'll have him ready to lead us out of this mess in four years.

But if I were graduating from high school today, I'd tell all these universities to stuff it and I'd go get a job mining uranium in Utah. The company is better. The conversation is better. And, most important, the education is better.

Okay, the *final* thing I'm gonna say about the American work force is that when it gets right down to it, nobody really wants you to succeed anyhow. When you succeed, it just reminds everybody else of whatever it is they *haven't* succeeded at. So we have this weird country where we talk about success all the time, we praise success, we encourage success, but we really don't like it when it turns up.

Here are the ten stages of American fame:

1. "He's a bright, young writer." (Meaning: You've never heard of him, so listen to *me*. I want credit for noticing him.)

2. "This is one of the finest first novels of the last twenty years, perhaps of the entire century." (Meaning: You've still never heard of him, but he's done something interesting, and I'm very hip because I'm talking about him.)

3. "His second novel, though not up to the quality of the first, shows a young genius struggling to find his place. Recently he's been seen in the company of Cher." (Meaning: Maybe he'll still be good copy this year, but I don't like him because too many other people like him.)

4. "In a remarkable development last week, he received a $10 million advance for his next three novels and a contract to produce his first novel as a major motion picture. In less than twenty-four hours, he became one of the ten richest writers in America." (Meaning: Nobody's that good. I hate him.)

5. "Sources within the New York publishing industry revealed that he missed three deadlines on his latest novel, and frittered away much of his vast fortune on an expensive drug habit and to settle his second divorce, to actress Kimberly Cantrell. When the first draft of his book was turned in, his editor was so distraught that the publisher is considering legal action. Could it be that, at the age of thirty-five, the Boy Wonder is already washed up?" (Meaning: He's rich. We can say anything. Fuck him.)

6. "Despite scathing reviews, his new book has remained on the *New York Times* best-seller list for seventy-four weeks. Obviously, you can never underestimate the taste of the American public. He had such a promising literary career before he started cranking out assembly-line schlock." (Meaning: He's too big for his britches. If the public likes him, he can't be any good.)

7. "He hasn't written a book in five years. What has happened to the once-famous playboy author who dined with princesses and was sought after by the largest publishing houses of the world? Some say he's moved to a villa in Switzerland and vows never to return to the country that took away his

private life. Others say he is recovering from nervous exhaustion brought on by his attempt to direct the screen version of his third novel. His friends are protecting his privacy, so no one can be certain just how shattered the man is." (Meaning: He hasn't given an interview in a long time. I like seeing him weak and confused. It makes me feel good.)

8. "After an absence from publishing of almost a decade, he has written one of the greatest books in the history of civilization. His appearance last week on *The Tonight Show,* gray-haired, bearded, and tanned, revealed a relaxed raconteur never before seen by the American public. Once a favorite of the gossip columnists, his career given up for dead by the tabloid press, he seems to have found a new public among the youth of America, who are rebelling against the values of their parents. The maturity of his work is like a breath of fresh air in a literary world obsessed with youth and novelty." (Meaning: He was gone long enough to be good copy again.)

9. "Today he was given a presidential medal and honored by the U.S. Congress as the most beloved man in American letters. The controversy and fire of his early career has been all but forgotten, especially by many of the young representatives, who weren't even born when his books were being banned from the public schools of the Midwest. Though he no longer writes novels, he told the press that he is working on a book of memoirs in three volumes. He is a symbol of America at its best." (Meaning: He's so old that he's no threat to any of us.)

10. "When they buried him yesterday, they buried a Literary Lion who should be taught in every classroom for the rest of eternity. He has no equals in this generation. Modern writing

is a small, paltry thing when compared to his greatness. The world has changed so much, but it was a better place when he lived and breathed—and wrote." (Meaning: He's dead, and I don't read.)

Finding Your Hairy Spear

A lot of people wonder why they don't find Iron Joe Bob earlier in their lives. They come up to me at the Wild Man Weekend and say, "Where were you twenty years ago, when I was married to Fishface Wilinsky?" Or "Where were you when I was investing in skunk ranches in Kuala Lumpur?"

And I have to explain to them that Iron Joe Bob doesn't just *show up*. You have to *need* him. You have to go through the testing of the Spear. You have to get your *cojones* ripped off a few times by the Dark Princess. You have to try the marriage deal, which, let's face it, was invented for *another* century, not this one. You have to go poking around Wall Street. And then, when you're ready, but not a moment before, Iron Joe Bob appears. And the first thing he does, of course, is screw your head on straight.

But the next thing he does changes your life even more:

Iron Joe Bob took the young brave's spear and he broke it across his knee, and the young brave wailed and

211

clutched his spear with both hands and bent over double in pain. But Iron Joe Bob spoke grimly to the brave, and he said, "Raise up your head, for I have a greater Spear, fashioned of gold, waiting for you in the Woolly Forest. But first you must do three things. You must become hairy. You must become hard. And you must become long." And the young brave said, "Would you repeat those, please?"

Hairy, hard, and long. What does the fairy tale mean?

To be "hairy" in the modern world means to let it dangle where it may. But it's a lot more than hair itself, even though hair itself is important. Ever wonder why everybody spends so much on Grecian Formula when the Kojak look is a lot sexier anyhow? It's because of the deep psychic need, the Iron Joe Bob crying out inside you, for wild hair.

You can even go to this store on East Thirty-eighth Street in New York City and buy a "detachable ponytail," the kind you can clip on the back of your head with bobby pins and hang down between your shoulder blades. The idea is, if you wanna look like a sixties folksinger or the producer of X-rated videos *but* you work in the mail room at the national headquarters of the Assembly of God in Springfield, Missouri, then you're gonna need some hair you can whip on and whip off at will. So this hairpiece company has come up with an eight-inch ponytail, real Italian human hair, for $299, and a twelve-incher for $499, and now even people in Sioux City, Iowa, can look like transvestites *any time they want to.*

Not that I have anything against ponytails. I've had three friends in my life who wore ponytails, and they all got away with it.

One was a guy named Mark who had an eight-inch handlebar mustache and used to smoke marijuana for breakfast in the early seventies. Mark is still famous at a small liberal arts college in Tennessee for being the guy who wrote his sociology term paper on "Why the Stones Are Better Than the Beatles"—and got an A on it! One day in the midseventies Mark mimeographed a letter to all his friends that said "Going to Ecuador—be back in 1984." And then he *came back* in 1984! Guys like this *should* wear ponytails, to distinguish them from the general population.

The second guy I met with a ponytail was Clarke Blacker, lead guitarist in a punk band called Stick Men with Ray Guns. People would jump up on the stage and try to spray-paint Clarke's guitar while he was playing, but Clarke knew how to drop-kick them into the third row and make them happy. Clarke became the musical director for my show, "An Evening with Joe Bob Briggs," when I added the Dancing Bovina Sisters, eight dancing girls with a combined weight of one ton. Clarke could hit a chord that was wide enough and muddy enough to make eight fat girls in tutus look like they could dance. Clarke's ponytail was short and purple. It was perfect. Clarke believed in the ponytail, so the ponytail worked for Clarke.

The third guy was Richard, a cable-TV producer who knows every restaurant and bar in New York, including some that won't open until 1994. TV guys always go one of two ways. The superhip, like Richard, have ponytails. The rest of em look like they just crawled up out of a Goodwill box. Stick a clipboard in their hands, give em a headset, clean a little moss off their teeth, and—*voila!*—they can produce the *ABC Evening News.* But the ponytail guys—especially the ones with pierced ears, like Richard—not only produce the TV shows. They believe TV is an art form. So these guys, obviously, are not playing with a full deck either.

Now what do we have in common here?

Ponytails belong to guys who . . . how can I put this? . . . to guys who are saying, "I can't cope, I can't deal with this, too much reality, I'm going to Ecuador, I'm slamdancing, I'm gonna make some video shows." Ponytail guys are in jobs where you don't have a water cooler, you don't have a desk, and sometimes—Mark's case—you don't even have a job.

So why would everybody, suddenly, start getting these phony ponies?

It can't be the reason men do *most* things—to get women. Most women don't care diddly about ponytails.

It *could* be a little yuppie guilt showing through, as in, "Once every ten years I should be a little spontaneous . . . I know! I'll organize my office! . . . No, something better . . . I'll grow my hair out! . . . No, too dramatic . . . I'll get a ponytail! . . . Someone might make fun of me . . . Wait! I've got it! I'll get a fake ponytail that I can store in my Day-Timer when I'm not using it!"

Or maybe . . . yeah, this is it, I've got it now . . . maybe everyone wants to be just like Howard Hesseman. Our role model for the nineties.

Anyhow, my point is: First thing, you've got to get hairy.

Making Your
Hairy Spear Hard

What is Iron Joe Bob talking about when he speaks of "getting hard"? What does it mean to "get hard" in today's culture?

I'm afraid we all *know* what it means. It means going to California.

I don't mean to "Go California." That's a different thing. You have to wear Japanese shirts to do that. What I mean is just go out to California, take a look around, say to yourself, "Okay, I get the idea, that's what the human body is *supposed* to look like if all you do is lift weights and drink pineapple juice." Then go back home and think about ways you get the approximate *result* of this without doing any actual work.

I don't recommend actually staying in California, because those people become so obsessed with the body it's all they can talk about.

I knew there was something wrong with my close personal friend, Rhett Beavers, starting two years ago when he finally got out of jail and moved to Grizzly Flats, California, to study hot-air ballooning. At one time Rhett was one of the biggest distributors of Arkansas Polio Weed in all of East Dallas, so it wasn't like him to just give up on his life's work and go scrape his brain against a sequoia like Sean Pean or somebody. He didn't even write to me. Course, he didn't know *how* to write, so that didn't bother me. But I missed him. I missed his aroma. I missed his calls in the middle of the night when he says, "Did I leave my TV set over there? I can't find it."

And so last week, when he showed back up, I didn't even recognize him at first. He'd finally shaved, for one thing. But he was also wearing a white smock down to his knees and Willem Dafoe sandals, and he said to me, "Brother Joe Bob—I call you brother because we are all sisters and brothers in the universe of beings—Brother, I am healed and ready to heal others."

Now I've been around TV shows enough lately to recognize some kind of Shirley MacLaine rock-worship deal when I hear it, but I wasn't exactly sure about this one.

"Rhett?" I said.

"Call me brother, Brother."

"Rhett, what are you?"

"I am an oral healer. At this very moment I would like nothing better than to clean your sickly incisors."

"You're a dentist?"

"I am a holistic dentist."

And it was true. Rhett had gone to this school in California where they turn out Mother Earth News dentists. Since he talked about it for three hours, I won't go into the whole deal, but the gist of it is that your mouth is all screwed up because your *head* is all screwed up, and if you'll twist your head back on straight, then your cavities will go away all by themselves. I'm not kiddin.

"Brother," he said, "have you ever considered why it is that you have so many cavities?"

"I always figured it was the five Mexican pralines a day that I eat, washed down with eight Budweisers."

"Exactly. As you can see, the cavity is the result, not of an excess of sugar, but of an eating disorder that is lodged in your psychological makeup. If we could change your heart—if we could remove the emotional polarization in your life—then we could clean your teeth."

"I thought Gleem was supposed to clean my teeth."

"You have much to learn, Brother. The chemicals that destroy your teeth come not from the candy. They come from the brain. Your very life is full of acid. That acid has to go somewhere."

"Lemme get this straight," I told him. "You're saying that something happens to me, like maybe I get ripped off on a couple of chrome exhaust pipes, and that starts my brain to going . . . "

"Irritation, anger, yes. Frustration. All those things manu-facture harmful acid in the brain."

"And then the brain starts shootin all this acid down into my mouth, and it eats up my choppers. In other words, it's not bacteria. It's brain-acid."

"Most men see the bacteria. But I have learned to look at the entire body, heart, and soul. When the heart and soul are lifeless, the bacteria have their way with you."

"So the brain-acid goes down there and tells the bacteria it's time to boogie."

"That is correct."

"You know something, Rhett? I understood you better when you had thirty, forty pounds of Arkansas Polio Weed in your hall closet."

"You got any?" Rhett said.

He was home at last.

I saved Rhett, but I can't save everybody. So the reason I

don't recommend going to California is that you start out to learn about your body, but it gets mixed up with all this weirdbeard muscle-worship head crud, and pretty soon you're going to Palm Springs five times a year to have Indians slap mud on your forehead with a stick.

California invented aerobics, too. Actually, a guy in the Canadian Air Force invented aerobics, but California *perfected* it. And now they're trying to make aerobics into an Olympic sport—long overdue, isn't it?—and people are getting so nutzoid over this that they're forming aerobic teams, hiring aerobics choreographers, nutritionists, personal trainers, and, of course, leotard handlers.

The way it works is, you have your aerobic competitor standing up in front of a panel of judges wearing her ankle-warmers, ponytail, and one of those Spandex pastel-pink bodysuits that makes her chest look like two Jell-O molds, and then she gives aerobics instruction to these *imaginary* aerobics students.

"Everybody on tiptoe now! Stretch and two and three and four, and *pull* and two and three and four, and *right arm* and two and three and four, and *another right arm* and six and seven and eight, now *grab those ankles with both hands and stick your head between your knees* and two and three and four and *raise one foot up off the ground and squeal like a wombat* and two and three and four and *squat on your neighbor* and six and seven and eight and *squat on your neighbor with the right buttock only* and two and three and four *now left buttock* and six and seven and eight *now both buttocks* and two and three and four *doesn't that feel good* and six and seven and eight . . . "

And this goes on forever while the judges are scoring the aerobics expert on "skill" (60 percent) and "presentation" (40 percent).

"I gave her a nine-point-four on skill. I especially liked the way she did the scissor extension crossover with her left leg while holding her stomach like a matador. But she got a nine-point-*nine* on presentation. She never stopped grinning. When she said 'Come on, *you can do it,*' I really *felt* something. I really *felt* she wanted those imaginary students to *achieve* something. Her musical selections were impressive as well. I've never heard 'Why Don't We Do It in the Road?' used for a postpregnancy workout. So a perfect ten for originality."

Actually, if they're gonna do this right, I think the competitors should be forced to perform in front of a room full of potbellied, cellulite-encrusted slugs who just enrolled in the class because somebody sold em a membership over the phone. Now *that's* adding some reality to the process.

You know how there's always one totally uncoordinated guy who, no matter how many times he's done the exercises, he's always *one* step behind the routine, but he never *knows* he's one step behind the routine, so you start watching this guy, hoping he'll catch up, or either get *so* slow that he catches up by mistake—are you following this?—but pretty soon *everybody* is watching him and so *everybody* starts messing up?

They should put one of these guys *right in front* of the competitor, with a cigarette hanging out of his mouth, dirty sweatshirt, high-top tennis shoes from 1967—and, of course, he wears *black socks* with his tennis shoes, Bermuda shorts with ducks and palm trees on em, or a Mexican shirt, one of those kind with all the pockets that fat people wear so they'll look skinny only they just look fatter—put one of these guys in the front row and *then* see how it works when they're grinnin and singin *"Work those deltoids* and two and three and four *you're looking good!* and six and seven and eight and *what's that big stain on your shirt?* and two and three and four and *that's disgusting!* and six and seven and eight and *work those fat folds* and two and three . . . "

Wouldn't this be more realistic?

So anyhow, no aerobics. I got into aerobics for a while, and I went so nutzoid that I started thinking I was an actual athlete. I was even thinking I might go out for this new sport called "triathlon."

You know how it works?

First you swim thirty-seven miles through icy, shark-infested water in nine-foot waves wearing one of those mono-buttocked wetsuits normally seen only in James Bond movies.

This is just the warm-up. After you've "rounded the buoy" and landed back on shore, you take off running, jump on one of those twenty-speed Italian bicycles with the wheels that look like dental floss, and then you pedal for 274 miles through quaint villages in the Swiss Alps. All the time you're doing this, you chug Evian yupster water out of a special "Evian Yupster Water Holder" plastic device attached to your bike.

Then, after you've cycled across the slopes of the Jungfrau, you jump off the bike and do a little fifty-nine-mile sprint to the finish line.

The first one to get out of surgery wins.

Who started this? Where is he? Isn't it time to scissor off this guy's hamstrings or something before he carries some automatic weapons up into the Empire State Building and starts hyperventilating?

I'm not kidding. All the guys that do this sport look like Bruce Dern. They got seventy-year-old men doing this sport. You know what a seventy-year-old Bruce Dern looks like? This is so far beyond jockdom we need a special word for it. It's not aerobics. It's not cybernetics. It's not dianetics. How about Psycho Sports?

It's the same principle as the guys who lift weights for so long that they look like they have muscles on the *outside* of their skin. The ones that always look like somebody just painted some linguini with tomato sauce on their stomachs. You see these guys and you think, "What if this is the day he does *one too many* bench-presses, and the whole thing pops open like a water balloon?"

These Psycho Sports Triple-Reverse Triathlon guys are the same way. They've got those giant veins in their foreheads from pumping their arms and bugging out their eyes while wearing supercool California goggle-shades. And when they fall down on the ground at the end of the race, grabbing their sides like maybe they're having three thousand appendicitis attacks at once, they're *happy*. They're looking at one another like, "Mine hurts worse!"

"Does not, mine hurts worse!"

"Well, my feet are bloody, nyah nyah nyah!"

"So what? I popped my shoulder out of its socket three times and lost all feeling in both thighs!"

And then, after they've compared notes like this for a while, they say, "Isn't this fun? I'm not really *that* serious about it, you know. I just do it to keep in shape."

"Oh, yeah, me, too. Love your purple leotard."

"Thanks. Do you think it really goes with the canary skullcap?"

"It's perfect. Come on. I've got to wind down. Let's go do some Icelandic snowshoe jogging."

"Great!"

Isn't there some way to execute these people all at once?

So forget all this *real* athlete stuff. That's *eighties* stuff. The word in the nineties is "low impact." Remember it. It could save your life.

One time when I was in San Francisco I met this couple, Brad and Trudy Brinker, who are the most up-to-date people I know in America. They're so up-to-date, they've already stopped using cellular phones and moved on to AT&T ear implants. They're so modern that they don't just go on fourteen-day wine-tasting vacations. They go on fourteen-day wine-*swimming* vacations, at their own fourteen vineyards, where they grow the grapes, make the wine, and print up the little menus with curlicues on em. These people are so trendy that they bought a house, but they didn't have time to live in the house, so they bought some people to live in the house *for* them. Have I made my point here?

Brad Brinker came over the other day to tell me how much his life is improving. Brad's life is always improving. One of these days Brad is just gonna go plumb up to heaven before he even dies, cause he just keeps improving so goldurn much. But this time Brad wanted me to know he's giving up jogging.

"High impact," Brad said. "Unhealthy."

Brad talks one breath at a time. It's some kind of weenie Zen deal I never have asked him about.

"But Brad!" I screamed at him. "You're the original Mr. Aerobic Hiney. You were jogging in seventy-two! Nobody jogged in seventy-two! Kenneth Cooper didn't jog in seventy-two! You have a shot at being obnoxious in three decades!"

Brad's been trying to get me to jog for about twelve years. The only exercise I've ever agreed to do is jerk the handle on a cigarette machine twice a day—you know, those metal kind that stick. I tell Brad it's "resistance training."

"Unhealthy," Brad said again. "Shin splints."

I noticed while Brad was talking to me that he had his pants hiked up under his armpits and his elbows stuck out behind him like a turkey in full strut.

"Brad, I noticed when you came in that you look like a piece of beef jerky on a string. Any reason for that?"

"I've taken up . . . " Brad said.

"I knew it was gonna be some new deal you've taken up. What have you signed up for now?"

"I've taken up walking," he said.

"Yeah?"

"That's it. Walking. Trudy's doing it with me."

"Y'all are gonna *walk* together?"

"Double walking. Double energy."

"Well, Brad, I think yall been doing that for a long time already."

"Power walking."

"Oh yeah, right, what's that?"

And then Brad proceeded to high-step around the room like the head drum major in the Grambling State University Marching Band, only it was kinda like the head drum major had a two-by-four strapped to his rear end.

"That's power walking?"

"Power walking," Brad said. "Very low impact. Very healthy."

"It looks to me like a sissy looking for dates at the mall, Brad."

"It's a very precise form of exercise," he said. And then he proceeded to tell me how he had elbow-and-hiney walkin shoes, elbow-and-hiney shorts, elbow-and-hiney fishnet shirt with his name on it, elbow-and-hiney knee pads—Brad had laid out about three hunnerd bucks for elbow-and-hiney walking equipment.

"I'll say one thing for it," I told Brad.

"What's that?" he said.

"It'll make people sorry to see you leave."

But even if you don't wanna go for the whole-hog elbow-and-hiney Brad Brinker turkey strut, you can still get a lot of mileage out of this "low-impact" stuff. What I would recommend, actually, is something called the Joe Bob Briggs workout. I got the idea from Jane Fonda.

The latest thing that Jane "Whoops! I'm Sorry!" Fonda forgot to tell us is that all her exercise videos of the eighties had the *wrong advice* on em. She used to tell people to "do it till your stomach burns," and now the doctors say people have been burning up their stomachs.

So Jane's into "low-impact" stuff now. Did you see her last year on *The Larry King Show* holding hands with Ted Turner and talking about her new low-impact, take-it-easy, don't-burn-yourself-up video? I almost expected her to say, "And one more thing—North Vietnam is full of Commie slimedogs! We should nuke the place!"

But I could have told Jane this eight years ago, when they first started selling the Abdomenizer on TV.

What do people want in an exercise plan?

Something that doesn't *feel like* exercise.

How much do people wanna hurt when they're exercising?

They *don't wanna hurt* when they're exercising!

And how much time a day do people wanna spend riding bikes and lifting weights and rearranging their hemoglobin on the joggin track?

Zero!

That's why, long before the "Body by Jake" Workout, long before the Raquel Welch "Get a Load of These Thighs" Workout, long before the Richard Simmons "Here's Another Neil Sedaka Record" Workout, and long before the Jane Fonda "You Won't Even Sweat" Workout, there was the Joe Bob Briggs "Five-Second Workout."

The Five-Second Workout is the ultimate exercise video for the nineties. Doctors now know that what it takes to be physically fit for the rest of your life is to work out three times a week, for twenty minutes each time. But who has that kind of discipline and self-control?

That's where my video comes in. Instead of spending twenty minutes of your valuable time on a rowing machine, you spend five seconds exercising, but you do it *720 times a week!*

The video includes 720 complete five-second workouts, and here's the beauty of this deal: Most of em are things you *already do anyway!*

IRON JOE BOB

Take Workout No. 364: Yanking the lever on the cigarette machine. If you pull it real slow, you'll gain five seconds of aerobic bicep benefit every time you do it.

Or how about Workout No. 278: Getting up to get the remote control off the top of the TV. All you have to do is *run* to the remote instead of walking. Two and a half seconds to get to the TV, two and a half to return, and if you lunge for the remote when you get there, you'll be working major muscle groups in the thighs and shoulders.

One of my favorites is Workout No. 448: Yelling at your girlfriend. The facial and vocal muscles are frequently overlooked when we plan an exercise regimen. Not with the Joe Bob Briggs Five-Second Workout! See how loud you're able to scream the following words, and be sure to time yourself: "They don't *make* panty hose that big, Rhinoceros Woman!"

Send me forty bucks today, and I'll send you the Five-Second Workout. Within six weeks, I guarantee you'll be attractive to most people living in Pine Bluff, Arkansas, or your money back.

Okay. You're hard now. You're hairy. But are you *long?*

Lengthening Your Spear

This may be hard for you to believe, if you've thought of yourself as having a short spear your whole life, but we're talking *attitude* here. If you *think* of your spear as long, it will become long. Or, as we used to say in Marine boot camp, "Find your manhood, and the rest of your body will go along for the ride."

You gotta have style, is what Iron Joe Bob is saying. And that means the first thing you gotta do is *get organized.*

I'll tell you another thing that'll surprise you. Sometimes I'm not a very organized individual. I know what you're thinking: "You? Joe Bob Briggs? The man that writes like a well-oiled dumptruck?" But yeah, it's true. Sometimes I lose things around the house, like the thermostat. I forget to go places I'm supposed to go, like to see my probation officer. I let my bar tabs stack up. In fact, there was a time when I would write books like this with no pants on. It was real embarrassing. In fact . . . whoops, excuse me . . . there, that's better.

That's why I wanna tell you about something that recently

changed my life, and let you know how it can change yours. Cherry Dilday, my personal assistant and ex-girlfriend, got me a device for Christmas called the Day Runner notebook for superorganized successful people, and it's already made me a more interesting person *and* a better writer.

What it is, is a blue-and-white looseleaf binder with seventy-four subdivisions in it, nine pockets, a ruler, a protractor, three condoms, and a Velcro snap. I carry this with me everywhere I go, except when I forget and leave it at home. But even if I get drunk and leave it somewhere, it wouldn't even matter, because of the first page in it, where I wrote down all my personal data: attorney's name, blood type, home phone numbers of ex-wives.

But the main part of the Day Runner organization system is these little colored stickers. They have a sticker for every single thing you could ever think of doing with your life. For example, I pick out five stickers representing aspects of life that are important to me—"Nightlife," "Sports," "Pleasure," "Trivia," and "Wines"—and then I grab hold of an orange plastic divider tab and I flip over to the back where it says "Objectives." Now. At the top of the first page, it says "Objectives This Month," and then it's divided into "Area of Interest: Career, Future, Self." So, for example, if I'm gonna state an objective, I just use one of the stickers—I'll choose "Wines." And then you've got to fill in underneath "Wines" what you're gonna *do* in the area of wines, or else you'll never get anything done in life. So I wrote "Drink them." But then you move on down the column under "Wines" to where it says "Benefits/Obstacles." That's where I wrote "Getting drunk"—actually, that could be a benefit *or* an obstacle, so it doesn't exactly work—but over on the other side of that same page it says "Steps." So I wrote in there "Go to liquor store." You see how this is simplifying my life? And then over next to that it says "When?" And so I wrote in "Get your hiney over there right now." And then it says "Priority?" with a check mark. So I put down "Pretty damn important." And so there is an example of one completed task in the Day Runner. I won't forget to get drunk on wine on February 4th.

But that's not all you can do with this mother. If you flip back to the front, it says "Projects," and this is for your long-term career planning. You just write in there some goal like "Win the Battle of the Monster Trucks," and then underneath it you describe "Plan of action":

"1. Get somebody to give me a big pile of money.

"2. Pay somebody to build me a truck.

"3. Buy one of those orange crash helmets with a chin strap."

But then you're probly thinking, "Okay, Joe Bob, but what happens after I get the master plan done, but then I can't remember what it is I'm trying to accomplish?" Easy! You cross-reference "Projects" with the section in the middle called "MEMO-RY," where you write in stuff like "Your wife's name is Susan, not Shirley." Then it has about fifty boxes to fill in under "MEMO-RY," and each box is . . . actually, I can't remember exactly what the "Memo-ry" section is for. I suggest you just rip that sucker out.

Now what have we learned today? We can find out the answer to that by turning to our tab index and flipping up the letter "L" for "Learn." And, that's interesting, it's blank! So, see, we've learned nothing today, but I think you know and I know that now, today, in this new decade, well, actually, it's not such a new decade anymore but I was late getting into it, it's time to get organized, get your life together, start some advance planning, get some objectives and some action agendas, spend all night doing your checkbook, so we can have some *fun* in the nineties.

Remember to write down all the fun *before* you have it, though.

IRON JOE BOB

The next thing you've got to do to perfect your new nineties male Iron Joe Bob attitude is to face up to all the mushy gooey stuff inside yourself that only women care about. I know this because last year I was on a lot of Communist-inspired talk shows along with all the psychologists who tell people how to have better relationships with their orthodontists and raise kids that won't commit mass murder or turn homosexual on em, and I met this one husband-wife psychiatrist team who were experts on how to have sex when you're fat, only they looked like they hadn't tried it lately, and they taught me how to start "humanizing" my relationships with my immediate family, even though most of my immediate family is perverted like me.

Are you following this? I hope so, cause I don't wanna have to say it again.

Anyhow, it dawned on me along about 9:30 a.m. in Denver—right after I finished my part of the show and right before the organic Zen burglar who got off cocaine by hypnosis was about to go on—it dawned on me that this "humanizing" deal is what's been wrong with me. All these years I had nonhumanized relationships. Like, to give you an example, take my ex-girlfriend Cherry Dilday. The reason it never worked out was I was kangaroo-izing the relationship. Part of the reason was Cherry Dilday had a face that looked like a kangaroo that got mashed flat on the interstate.

Another thing I realized about my life is how I'm afraid of my sexual feelings. This one was explained to me in Seattle by Dr. T. Emmett Scranton of Frankfort, Kentucky, the world-renowned expert on the sexually handicapped. Dr. Scranton told me that my obsession with 38 triple-D's is actually a desire to be rolled into a doughnut and dunked by a Lily Tomlin look-alike. Now that I know this, I'm trying to flex my psychosexual libido and circumnavigate my navel.

But here's the biggie. It happened in Cleveland while I was

rappin with Dr. Sullivan Sturges of the Betty Ford Brain Research Center, and Dr. Sturges stopped me in my tracks when he diagnosed my "psychopathia El Chico digestibus," which is a very serious brain disorder caused by eating too many frozen Meskin TV dinners. Fortunately, I have the mild form, caused by consuming an average of thirty-eight burritos a week, and not the Class A version, which involves actually crossing the Meskin border, finding a Meskin chef, and saying, "I'll have one of them goat burgers, *por favor.*" This more serious type frequently includes massive gunshot wounds and missing cars. All I can say is, I immediately went in for tests, got my brain flushed out and sucked dry, and I feel like a new man.

Once I *became* a new man, I found out that I was naturally a *nasty* person. Isn't the voyage of self-discovery a wonderful thing? I'll show you what I mean:

Have you ever had something happen to you that just made you want to cry out, "Why? My God, why? Why me?"

Of course you have. Maybe it was that year you slashed all the tires on your Little League coach's car, and a week later you got a brand-new bicycle. Or maybe it was the time you spread it around the office that your boss was a Satanic cultist and baby murderer, and right after that your boss got fired and *you* got a promotion. You may have wondered about this at the time. You may have said, "Huh?"

That's why you need a copy of my new pamphlet, "When Good Things Happen to Bad People."

Let's take the case of eighty-nine-year-old Werner Streubel, a concentration-camp warden responsible for the deaths of 950,-000 people during World War II. Werner's only remark: "I enjoyed every one of them." Where is Werner today? He's chairman of the board of the Seabreeze Yacht and Tennis Club in the Fiji Islands, living under the name Warren Smith. He's *the only one they never found out about.* Now at first glance you may think, "God is not being fair here." You may try to blame this on somebody other than yourself. But hold on a minute. I want you to start thinkin back over your entire life, and think of *every single time you got away with it.*

See what I mean? Do you *really* want Warren to fry? Do you *really* want God to start keepin score? No. Of course you don't. What you really want is to *keep getting away with it.*

That's where the pamphlet comes in. Did you ever wonder why it is that your banker, who never loans you any money, rips you off on your service charges, and won't clear your checks on time, always lives to be ninety-four and gets fabulously wealthy, while you have to keep running down to the bank to cover your checks all your life? It's this easy:

That banker, who has probly read my pamphlet, starts every day by doing *one nasty thing.* That's all it takes. Just one. He might purposely take ten bucks out of somebody's checking account so it won't balance at the end of the month. He might send a note to one of his business partners' wives telling her that her husband is having an affair with a herpes-infested real-estate agent. Or, if he's not feelin up to a lot of mental work, he might just park his car sideways across three spaces so nobody else can park that morning. Whatever it is, it automatically makes him a *bad person.*

Do you see the beauty here? He *knows* he's a bad person. He doesn't have to worry about it anymore. And what's everybody else doing? They're out there trying to be *good.* And so you know what happens to them? Their friends keep callin em up all the time to be picked up at the airport. Do you think this banker ever picks anybody up at the airport? Forget it. He's too *bad.* Nobody *wants* him to pick em up at the airport.

Once this system starts workin for you, there's no end to it. When you get into the advanced lessons, you'll learn such exciting fields as rip-off 800-number telemarketing, aluminum siding sales, and, of course, TV evangelism. And then you, too, will know why good things happen to baaaaaad people.

Hostility will be a major trend in the nineties. I learned this from Brad and Trudy Brinker, who I mentioned before as the most up-to-date couple in America.

The latest thing that Brad and Trudy did is they went for six days to Big Sur to a Creative Primal Divorce Encounter. This stuff is so far beyond est, you have to have an American Express platinum card just to order the brochure. What it is, all these couples go out in the woods and have a ceremony where they recite some Indian poetry and symbolically divorce one another. Then they let that set in for three, four days. Let's face it, you've just turned loose fifty, sixty people that've been married for a combined total of four hundred years, what do you *think* is gonna happen? These people are out there Significant-Othering their brains out.

Then they get a Unitarian priest to come in and show a porno video while they sit with their original partners and communicate about what turns them on about Marilyn Chambers' body. Then the Unitarian guy sends em back into the woods to write down sentences in spiral notebooks that start out "One thing I've never told you about myself is . . . " Or "One thing I can't stand about you is . . . "

And then the answers are stuff like "You remember that time I went to Fort Worth and you thought it was weird? Well, it was weird. Boy, was it weird. She was 105 pounds of Kinko City. I shoulda told you, but I was chicken." And then you take your spiral notebook and you give it to your Significant Other, and he or she takes it off into the woods by him or herself and writes an answer in there like "You need professional help, jerk!" And then the Unitarian priest brings you back together in a giant therapy group where you can go through the Primal Divorce proper, screaming at each other like weasels being sliced up in a coffee grinder.

Once this is over, you both cry for a long time. Crying is very important. "Brad cried five different times during the week," Trudy told me. "The next best husband only cried three times."

And then they all have some apple juice and talk about the sexual urges they had when they were eight years old but were too embarrassed to tell anybody but now they can. And then they hug. Hugging is very important. And then they all go out for cappuccino. Cappuccino is very, *very* important.

And then they all bid fond farewells and head for home, where they are renewed, refreshed, alive again, and they start lying to one another with a clean slate.

I find this stuff fascinating.

We accomplish the same thing in one hour at the Wild Man Weekend, though, by having a big lesbian girl named Martha come and beat the stuffings out of you.

Now. Don't forget what we're doing here. We're lengthening the spear. We're trying to make that spear last longer. We're taking a little boy's spear and turning it into a man's spear. Because think about it for a minute—what is it that makes a man's spear go bad on him?

That's right. He's afraid of getting old. And the Baby Boom yupster is *especially* afraid of getting old, because he's lived thirty, forty years under the illusion that nobody ever *gets* old. So now we're starting to see the results of it.

Now that all these books are coming out, like *It's Okay to Be Real Old* and *So You're Seventy—Who Cares?* and *Tips on Living to Be 170 and Enjoying Most of It*—in other words, now that people have been to so many aerobics classes they think they're immortal—I decided to go see Chubb Fricke, the oldest guy I know, and see what he knows about it. Chubb is the oldest living PBA bowler. In fact, every year the PBA sponsors four major tournaments: the PBA Champeenship, the PBA Seniors Champeenship, the PBA "Golden Age" Seniors Champeenship, and the PBA Chubb Fricke Tournament. The Chubb Fricke Tournament consists of Chubb getting up out of his chair, walking to the foul line, and bowling one ball. If it stays out of the gutter, he wins. That's how old Chubb Fricke is.

So anyhow, I went over to Chubb's house, which is where he's lived for the last fifty years and he still complains about what it cost him last time he moved, and I said, "Chubb, what's your secret?"

And Chubb said, "Never tell em you're married."

And I told him, no, that's not what I'm talking about. "What's your aging secret? How'd you get to be so old and you can still remember your name?"

Chubb thought about that for a minute. Then he cleared his throat, adjusted himself in his chair, cleaned his glasses, brushed his teeth, ordered a pizza, and placed a bet on the seventh race at Louisiana Downs. You ever notice how when you ask an old person a real important question, they have to go through three hours of getting ready to answer?

Finally, Chubb was ready.

"Joe Bob, I never gave a flip."

"I *know* you don't give a flip, cause you're *old,* but I wanna know how you got to *be* so old."

"I'm telling you," Chubb said. "Listen to me, I never *gave* a flip. That's the secret. That's it. That's all there is."

"What do you mean that's all there is?"

"That's all there is. Don't give a flip, and you'll live a long time."

"What about exercise, diet, marital relationships, pensions?"

"Nope. Except you shouldn't give a flip about em. Worry about exercise and diet all the time, you'll die early."

"What about smoking?"

"Look at the great smokers who live sixty, seventy years after they start. You know why?"

"I can guess."

"They don't give a flip. They don't smoke for fifteen years and then start *worrying* about smoking for the *next* fifteen years and then quit smoking and spend the fifteen years after that worrying about whether they quit smoking *soon enough.*"

"So that's it? That's everything?"

"Bowling helps—but only if you don't give a flip. *Wheel of Fortune* is good, but only the daytime version. At night there's too much money—you start giving a flip. Daytime version of *Wheel of Fortune,* sometimes I yell for the wheel to land on 'Bankrupt.' But let me put it this way, Joe Bob. You know how you meet all those mean people in life that cheat you on the interest and stab you in the back on business deals and fire you when you don't deserve it?"

"Yeah. Heavy stress for them, right?"

"Nawwwww. That's who I learned it from. They all live to be ninety-six, don't they? And you know why? They don't give a flip. Don't give a flip about you, don't give a flip about their wife— they don't give a flip."

"That's very inspiring, Chubb."

"You asked me how to live a long time. I didn't say you could sell it to the movies."

That's enough wisdom from the mind of Chubb Fricke for now. Let's leave him ruminating to himself and move on.

Searching for the Woolly Forest

And after a time the young brave's eyes were opened and he saw that his Golden Spear was hairy, and it was hard, and it was long. And he said to Iron Joe Bob, "I think I'll stay here all day." And Joe Bob commanded him to put away his spear. "It may not be used until you have found the Woolly Forest." And the young brave asked, "But where is the Woolly Forest." And Iron Joe Bob said, "It appears when you least expect it, so keep that spear ready at all times."

What do you think Iron Joe Bob is talking about here? I think it's fairly obvious that some kind of spiritual search is going on. Like most people, the young brave starts out in a conventional place. He's a spiritual baby. He's wearing a loincloth, he's alone in the forest, what can he possibly know? And this is where we all start our spiritual journey—in a dirty, dark place where everybody knows the rules but us. In other words, it starts in church.

I'm a Babtist, so I know all about this. In fact, I've attended every meeting of the Southern Babtist Convention since 1974. This year's convention down in San Antone was attended by 39,417 saved people and one person who's going to hell. He snuck in. We respect his right as an individual to be eternally damned.

As you know, every year I report on what we do down there, and this year I was attending as the messenger of the Church Under the Rock of Grapevine, Texas, where our motto is "No checks accepted without six forms of I.D."

We had two main issues to talk over this year. The first one was:

If ever single Babtist can interpret the scriptures exactly like the Lord tells him to, then what about people that are dumber than dirt?

After seventeen hours of debate—and most of it was devoted to unfortunate people in state institutions for the feeble-minded and reetards—we prayed for liquid refreshment and then came up with the answer:

God intended for whoever has the highest, slickest pompadour in church to decide what's right. So if you don't listen up and pay attention to the man, your hiney is going straight to the eternal Western Sizzler Steakhouse.

This decision was so controversial that 250 members of the Third Babtist Church of East Fallopian Tube, Tennessee, marched down to the Alamo and ripped up the holy decision and sang a song about a demon named Elmo. We ignored em, though, cause they were blow-dryed.

But the main issue at this year's convention got reported out of committee at the very end, and it went like this:

"Are Catholics and Jews and Hairy Krishnas all going to hell just like drug-head Communist atheistic unemployed slimeballs? Or do they have a shot at salvation?"

And we finally got an answer on this one—we been debating this one for so many years it was good to finally hear from the Big Guy—and the answer was:

"We respect the rights of non-Babtist jerks everywhere to reject the Babtist God and bring racking pains onto their bodies as they are lifted onto the devil's torture rack and sliced into a thousand pieces so that their bodies bleed forever but they never die, they just burn and bleed, burn and bleed, cry out in agony, suffocate, suffer, moan, and beg to be back on earth where they could throw all their Coors out and only drink milk. Of course, if they become Babtists before they die, then never mind."

Every year we always pass a few amendments to the Ten Commandments, too, but the only one you might be interested in, since you might not be a Babtist and might not understand how hopeless your situation is, is Ten Commandments Amendment Number 1,345:

"Thou shalt love thy neighbor unless he's a snot-nosed teenager who throws stuff in your yard for pure meanness."

I love being Babtist.

But after a while, a young man—even a devoted Babtist young man like myself—starts to stray a little bit, think about other possible alternatives, think about trying one of the religions that seems to have more of a *future* in it.

Like going Catholic. For a while, a couple years ago, I decided I'd be a Catholic priest. Most of yall know that I been looking for a decent job for years. And they were *begging* people to take this job. They've got seventy-five million Catholics in the USA, the churches are getting huger and huger, and the number of priests is getting smaller and smaller, and now they got Holy Fathers out there on the recruiting trail, showing film strips to high school seniors, asking new priests to "bring a friend" down to the office and "try on this here dog collar." They're desperate.

Up in Chicago, they're even willing to pump up the salaries

a little bit, because priests have been dropping like flies. They've lost so many priests up there that they now have Catholic MPs that patrol up and down Michigan Avenue on weekdays, rousting runaway clergy out of advertising agencies. Ever since Pope John Paul the Sequel got into office, it's been crystal clear that the number one priestly rule-change was *never* gonna get past the Holy Unified Committee of Senile Bishops. You know which rule I'm talking about:

No nookie.

Back in the sixties and seventies, it was starting to look good for the old ecclesiasticus aardvarkus, if you know what I mean and I think you do. The priests and nuns figured, "We'll swing with this a few more years, and maybe they'll at least let us marry some ugly Pakistani women or something."

But John Paul His Polishness pretty much wiped that out when he said: No nookie for priests. No abortion. No birth control. No premarital sex. And the guys in Chicago tried to reason with him, but they got an idea of just how serious he was when he ordered several countries in Southeast Asia to be spayed and neutered.

So that's a drawback. That's uncool.

But not for me—because *I never have sex anyway.*

You see the beauty here? Through the majesty of God's plan, you take something that's *embarrassing* and it becomes an *asset.* You can say stuff like, "See that Raquel Welch look-alike over there with the high heels who's wearing the bra on the outside of her dress? Yeah, her—the one that's working the Etch-a-Sketch with her thighs. Now, see the Kevin Costner look-alike who just walked up to her and is now touching her waist? I want you to know something: That no longer bothers me—because *I couldn't have her anyway.*"

Isn't this great?

Okay, what's the next one?

Poverty.

Perfect. I love poverty. The church pays for the food. You wear the same clothes every day. And you still get a check! But you don't have to be responsible. You don't have to save up for the little rug-rat's college education. You don't have to buy party dresses for the wife. That leaves the *whole check* for beer, topless bars, and entry fees when you wanna run your Nissan Hardbody SE Four-by-Four in the weekend drags.

Then we got—oh yeah—obedience. Or, as we say in Latin, "shutta yo mouth." This is the easiest one of all. Here, I've been practicing:

"Yes sir, Mr. Archbishop sir, I do believe, sir, that the Pope is infallible. I know this because, in 1870, the Pope decided he was infallible. He told everyone he was infallible, and so, if he *was* infallible, then he couldn't be wrong *deciding* he was infallible, because that was his first infallible act, to declare himself infallible . . . Of course, the year before that, in 1869, the Pope was full of dog doo."

"Yes sir, Mr. Archbishop sir, I think God did intend for us to use the rhythm method of birth control. Yesterday I counseled one of my parishioners to mark his calendar and set his alarm clock to throw caution to the winds and rip his wife's clothes off on the 24th at 9 p.m. They're quite looking forward to it."

And, of course, I've been preparing for this job for years. I saw the original *Exorcist* thirty-four times. I watched every single Bing Crosby movie where he was a Catholic priest who sang ballads. And I was the first person on earth to review the most famous drive-in double feature ever programmed—and, I can see now that it was a Roman Catholic twin bill: *I Drink Your Blood* and *I Eat Your Skin.*

I'm ready. Take me. Bless me, Father, for now that I've written this, I won't be able to go to Chicago for at least eight years.

IRON JOE BOB

I eventually gave up almost *all* organized religion, though, due to my experiences in the Holy Land. And actually I think that's what made me realize that you don't find the Woolly Forest in the church house.

It started when everybody at the Church Under the Rock got tired of just talking in tongues and eating tuna casseroles ever Wednesday night, so one Christmas we chartered a Greyhound and went to the Holy Land for the holidays to get some peace on earth. It was great.

First we went to the Wailing Wall and watched some guys in pigtails act like sissy slamdancers.

Then we went to the Church of the Baby Jesus in Bethlehem and watched a Greek Orthodox priest hit an Armenian priest over the head with a broom handle cause it was *his* turn to hose down the manger. I bought a Baby Jesus paperweight snow scene.

Then we went down to the Dome of the Rock and watched some Muslims kiss the dirt. I bought a digital watch.

Then we went to the Jaffa Gate, the Damascus Gate, St. Stephen's Gate, Golden Gate, Zion Gate, and the Dung Gate. At the Dung Gate I bought another paperweight.

Then we went to the Dead Sea and floated around in it until we got goo on our faces and threw up.

Then we went to Tel Aviv and watched some guys with Uzi submachine guns talk about how the terrorists will come and bomb the elementary schools. I bought an Uzi submachine gun.

Then we went out in the desert and watched some really ugly ladies make a rock garden and rap about how great it is to be livin in a dirt hut instead of their New York apartments. I bought some holy dirt.

Then we went to the Monastery of the Flagellation and watched a Catholic monk flagellate a Russian Orthodox altar boy. I bought a bullwhip.

Then we went to the River Jordan and watched some Palestinians spit on some Jews.

Then we went to the Lebanese border and asked some soldiers where Danny Thomas was from. I bought an Uncle Tanouse bathrobe.

Then we went to the big Jerusalem Holy Day Parade and watched all the Babtists, Roman Catholics, Greek Orthodoxes, Russian Orthodoxes, Methodists, Armenian Apostolics, Hasidims, Druzes, Conservative Jews, Orthodox Jews, Reform Jews, Sephardic Jews, Mennonites, Lutherans, Nazarenes, Disciples of Christ, Congregationalists, Quakers, Unitarians, Syrian Jacobites, East Syrians, Coptics, Ethiopian Orthodoxes, Pentecostals, Adventists, Jehovah's Witnesses, Hutterites, Moravians, Christian Scientists, Mormons, Brethren Churches, Christians of Saint Thomas, Nestorians, Bulgarian Orthodoxes, Cyprus Orthodoxes, Georgian Orthodoxes, Serbian Orthodoxes, Anglicans, Episcopalians, Welsh Protestants, Primitive Babtists, Free Methodists, Wesleyans, Shakers, Christadelphians, Bible Churches, African Methodists, Hussites, Taborites, Assemblies of God, Jesus Onlys, Cumberland Presbyterians, Dutch Reformeds, Evangelicals, and Chaldean Catholics march in tribute to the one true God.

I bought a money clip.

Obviously, we're still a long way from the Woolly Forest.

Entering the Dry Brushy Area at the Edge of the Woolly Forest

The legend continues:

When the young brave stopped staring at his own Golden Spear and looked up, he saw that the Woolly Forest had been there all the time. He said, "But how could I have not seen it till now." And Iron Joe Bob replied, "You were standing there with your spear in your hand."

What an apt metaphor for the spiritual condition of modern man. We stand there with the spear in our hand, and all the time the Woolly Forest of our dreams is just a few feet away.

I think the journey into the forest proper begins when we take direct action to help the spirit.

You probly remember how a few years back I drove up to Tulsa to get some spiritual advice from Oral Roberts and ask him to raise my career from the dead, but when I got there he wasn't available and so I had to talk to Oral's unsaved half-brother, Anal Roberts. It was a moment that changed my life. Ever since then the two of us, Anal and I, have had a weekly radio ministry on a three-station network out of Shelby, Montana, where we ask people to send in all their money so that someday we'll have enough to build an actual radio station in Shelby.

Well, we need $400 million. I'm not gonna sugarcoat it. I know it sounds like a lot, but do you know what might happen if everbody reading this book don't get up off their hineys right now and send me $400 million? I do. God appeared to me in a vision last night and he *told* me what's gonna happen if Anal and me don't get the four hundred mill:

"I will allow Oral Roberts to live forever."

I tried to reason with the Big Guy. I tried to tell Him He was makin the biggest mistake of His Life. But he wouldn't budge.

"No way, José," said God. "Either you get the cash or Oral gets Methusalized. I may not kill him off for *at least* seven, eight centuries."

Now is this really what we want? After all, this is what the guy's been shootin for. Oral says if you get a disease or a broke head, then all you got to do about it is pray real hard and ask God to make you look like Jack La Lanne, and this is the reason there are so many 650-year-old billionaire Christians hangin around Tulsa today.

Finally I was able to get one little concession out of God.

"Okay, okay, okay, if you get the money in *two months*," He told me, "then I'll take Oral off your hands. I'm not *promising*. At this point I'm saying it's just a strong possibility that I could, you know, arrange a little accident during choir practice, something like that."

"Something involving a soprano?"

"I'm not *promising* the Soprano Treatment, now just stop it, that's the last I want to hear on the subject."

So there you have it, and I think you can see what's put before us. Two months. Four hundred mill. Make the checks out to "Joe Bob Briggs Tax-Free Evangelistic Radio Ministry," and make *sure* that at the bottom of every check you write either "Thumbs Up" or "Thumbs Down." Don't worry about gettin the spelling right. God will know what you mean.

But Anal Roberts was just the beginning of my nontraditional spiritual trek. It was shortly after that that I got seriously into astrology. In fact, it was around the same time that Nancy Reagan started getting creepy on us. I became so good at doing star charts that people all over Grapevine would come by the trailer house just to find out what was gonna happen to em in their life. I never did charge any money for it, though, cause it was depressing telling people all day long they were gonna die some day.

Anyhow, just to show you how I'm still in touch with my moon phases, here's today's Joe Bob Briggs Horrorscope:

ARIES (March 21–April 19): You'll want to stay in bed until 3 p.m. Someone at the office will say "Where'd you get that hickey on your lip?" There's an excellent chance that you will die soon.

TAURUS (April 20–May 20): You've been evasive lately and people are noticing. Enter the Federal Witness Protection Program. Your chart promises excitement, but only when nude in public. A good time to eat red meat and switch the buttons on your car radio.

GEMINI (May 21–June 20): Your attention centers on a person of the opposite sex. Look for some excitement and changes in your life. You are probably a homosexual.

CANCER (June 21–July 22): All of those money problems will be solved soon. Time to make that decision about your dwelling place and your legal affairs. The next three days are a good time to buy a handgun. If you feel nauseous any day this week, you have cancer.

LEO (July 23–Aug. 22): Don't be surprised if you feel like you woke up in a sitcom. CBS is about to offer a contract! You are perceived as powerful, secure, and in control. They're suckers, aren't they?

VIRGO (Aug. 23–Sept. 22): On the inside you feel like Jell-O. On the outside you *look* like Jell-O. Go to the health spa for a facial and body wrap.

LIBRA (Sept. 23–Oct. 22): Your lunar aspect highlights sensuality, travel, a stranger with a mole on his or her inner thigh, and a nonalcoholic piña colada. Soon one of your friends will start saying things behind your back and you'll have to be a jerk about it.

SCORPIO (Oct. 23–Nov. 21): Time for a fresh start and a new look. Refuse to bathe today and dye your hair a pastel color. A former teacher will come back into your life and laugh at your britches.

SAGITTARIUS (Nov. 22–Dec. 21): You must get to the heart of the matter today. Pay attention to anyone who has a Japanese name, especially if they seem real stupid. At the office, no one will be watching the petty cash fund.

CAPRICORN (Dec. 22–Jan. 19): Good day to kill anyone named Jennifer or Brad. Otherwise, plant yourself on the couch for the day and imitate a garden vegetable.

AQUARIUS (Jan. 20–Feb. 18): You have lost the Publishers Clearinghouse Sweepstakes. Nyah nyah nyah. Good day to cancel all the magazine subscriptions that didn't do you a damn bit of good.

PISCES (Feb. 19–March 20): Moon in your sign corresponds to a deep secret about *that thing* that you did as a kid. *Everyone* is going to find out. You can't avoid it. The whole *world* is going to know. You'll be *humiliated*. Good day to start a hobby.

I tried to sell my horoscopes to the newspapers, but they never would buy em. I don't know why.

Anyhow, that's not the point. The point is that astrology was sort of the jumping-off place that got me started toward the true inner meanings of things. But the thing that really cinched it was when Wanda Bodine got drunk one night and ordered the complete *Mysteries of the Unknown* series from Time-Life Books.

Ever since then Wanda has been predicting her Harmonious Heart Path. For a while, when we were back in the *Visions and Prophecies* book, Wanda would dangle a rock on a key chain and then ask it a question. If the key chain rotated clockwise, it meant "Yes." Counterclockwise meant "No." This is how she ended up buying seven pairs of leopard-print high heels.

Then one month the *Portents in the Palm* book came in the mail, and for a long time I had to stick my hand out every time I wanted a beer.

"Joe Bob, your Fate Line says you will remain active and intellectual all your life," she'd tell me, "and so you'd better not *screw it up* by drinking a beer."

And I told her, "The reason I have that line permanently pressed in my hand is from squeezing thousands of beer cans around the tin ridge. It's absolutely *necessary* to my future that I have a beer."

By then, I was starting to believe in this stuff.

Next came *Penmanship and Personality,* the one about how your handwriting reveals the secret to your soul. And so I wrote out the Gettysburg Address one night for Wanda, so she could analyze it, and after a while she said, "Joe Bob, you're not in the book."

And I said, "What do you *mean,* I'm not in the book? Everbody's in the book."

But she said there was nothing in the book about a person's writing where every other letter slants in a different direction and every tenth letter is upside down. But there has *got* to be a meaning to stuff like that. That doesn't just happen by *accident.*

Psychic Powers showed up one day, and—here's the really strange part—I had this *premonition* that we were gonna get a book about psychic powers.

Also—you know, these things start adding up—Wanda had a premonition, too. She had a premonition that one day she would go out and buy seven purses to match her seven pairs of leopard-print high heels. And, sure enough, she *did.*

But the one that takes the cake is *Numerology,* the one we just got. If you take the name Joe Bob Briggs and figure out the true numeric meaning of it, here's what you get:

Soul Number: The essence of my soul is three. I normally have three dollars stuffed way down in my pocket. I have three good tires on my car. I bum an average of three cigarettes a day. Three of my ex-wives still get money from me. These are things that only *I* could know about myself. Pretty amazing.

Outer Personality Number: The way others see me is nine. When I go to the drive-in bank, they have to yell over the intercom "Sir, may I help you?" exactly nine times before I answer. When I play golf, my average score on each hole is nine. And, most incredible of all, I wear the same nine shirts over and over again.

Path of Destiny Number: My future is two. I will marry only two more women in my lifetime. I will be sued only two more times. I will begin a weight-training program and work up to two repetitions a day. And my great hope for the future is that someday I will bet the 2-2-2-2-2-2 Super-fecta "Pick Six" at Louisiana Downs racetrack and then I can retire.

There was a time when I would have *laughed* at this stuff.

Penetrating Deep into the Wet Woolly Forest

When the moooooooon is in the seventh house,
And Jupiter aligns with Maaaaaars,
Then people who go on Donahuuuuuuue
Will haaaaave sex with Mason jars,
This is the dawning . . .

Of course you know *exactly* what I'm talking about.

It's the moment we're all waitin for. The moment when the young brave enters the mysterious depths of the Woolly Forest for the first time:

> *The young brave, now plunging wildly through the brush, suddenly arrived at the exact center of the forest in a clearing moist with dew, but as soon as he did, there appeared a huge writhing monster, blocking his way. The young brave raised his Golden Spear without thinking and plunged it into the monster repeatedly, deeper and deeper, slow at first, then faster, and the monster began to give way.*

Isn't this a strange direction for our tale to take? What to make of it?

Obviously we're into deep Shirley MacLaineville here.

I'll never forget the day I first met Shirley myself: August 17, 1987.

Remember the day the New Age Movement people all jumped in their BMW love sedans, motored their hineys out to Idaho, and waited for the exact moment when the Aztec calendar, which is aligned with the Mayan calendar and the Russian Orthodox thirteenth-century hickey-removal calendar, all came to a dead stop during a total eclipse of the dog star, Fido?

We were all packed, we'd sold our houses and everything, cause when it happened the spaceships were gonna come, with Wyndham Hill piano music seepin out of their stereo systems like we got trapped in a Marin County wine-spritzer social, and the outer-space Coneheads were gonna get out and tap us gently on the shoulder to adjust our psychic awareness of interplanetary Tantric Yoga travel and we would be, like, vaporized into the giant automatic teller machine of the heavens or else Jesus Christ would get out of a 426 Hemi Cuda and say "Yo."

We weren't sure about the details, and obviously, as it turned out, we weren't sure about the date, either. But now we are. We made a few adjustments, based on an Aztec god named Terwilliger who screwed up in the ninth century and left several years off the calendar, and now we *do* know the exact date. It's April the 5th of next year.

I know that a lot of you still have some minor doubts about this. You're still not sure just who to believe. So I wanna run down the list of the most frequently asked questions:

1. Where should I go on the 5th?

A. We're building a Navel Observatory in Idaho.

2. Why Idaho?

A. The aliens are heading straight for Boise. We don't know why. We think it has something to do with potato farming.

3. Wasn't the calendar already supposed to end in 1974, and then again in 1987, and then again in 1989?

A. Yes, but we got it extended one more time for fund-raising purposes.

4. Why do we use the Mayan calendar to calculate the dawning of the "new age"?

A. Because the Mayans achieved the highest civilization in the history of the world. They were the first people to do stuff like eat human hearts, build rock piles in Lima, eat donkey dung—stuff like that.

5. How do we know we got the right calendar date this time?

A. We used to think all the Mayans were dead, but now we think they just married Meskins. We found a guy named Antonio Pepe Espinoza de la Acapulco, also known as the Black Butcher of Yucatan, who claims to have a calendar that's been in the same place for 3,500 years, and there's a whole lot of X's marked over the numbers on it. We took the new findings to Antonio and proposed April 5th as the end date.

6. And what did Antonio say?

A. *"Vamos à la Boise."*

7. And what exactly *will happen when we get there?*

A. We'll get all these people in one place, smash their Sony Walkmans, and we'll *never* have to listen to that wind-and-surf treefrog music ever again.

Now that I've got that straightened out, I wanna get back to my main point, which is how I met Shirley MacLaine:

A long time ago, in my fifth past life, I was an Indonesian bamboo stripper named Felix and I worked for the Rajah of Punjab. I got 340 magpies for working a sixteen-hour day, but I didn't mind because at night I would get to go home to my clay hut and play with my pet weasel. The weasel's name, it turns out, was Shirley MacLaine.

"Shirley," I would say, "what were you before you were a weasel?"

And Shirley would say, "Moogl moogl moogl."

This is the only sound a weasel can make.

So then I would go and get the village witch doctor, Clarence the Witch Doctor, and Clarence would come over and stuff Shirley into an earthen jar and bang on the side until it was revealed to Clarence who the weasel was in his past life, and on some nights Ramtha would come out of the jar and we'd shoot the breeze talkin about what a bummer it was that you can't understand what those people from Atlantis are saying cause they have so much water in their lungs, and then sometimes, if we were real lucky, Ramtha would charge us 4,800 magpies an hour (300 modern dollars) and predict the future.

"Someday this weasel will have many jerk boyfriends," said Clarence in broken Indonesian. And then there was a mighty whoosh of wind and Ramtha jumped out and said, "Yeah, but she can take five gross points and a back-end pay-or-play talent contract on the miniseries rights."

And then Ramtha went into this long deal about how this wasn't just any ordinary weasel. Some day this weasel would put on a canary-yellow jumpsuit and run around pinning Jerry Lewis against the wall and planting kisses all over his face. And then after that the weasel would put on some pink underwear and start kicking the backside of Juliet Prowse's dress in *Can-Can*. And then after that she would join the Rat Pack and make a bunch of movies where she gets to scrunch up her eyes and squeal a lot. And then she'd go to Tibet and sit on top of a mountain and not shave her legs for a week. And then she'd buy a place in Malibu and put in a hot mineral bath where she could meditate about life and how much she can't stand Debra Winger. And then she'd go to South America and start yelling out, "I am God, I am God," until somebody snatched up the paperback rights, and then, of course, she'd be one of the great spiritual leaders of herself of all time.

After I got finished ramming seventeen punji sticks through the weasel's throat and watching it die a long, slow, agonizing death, Ramtha promised me all the danger was gone. All I had to do was remember *one* simple little thing:

Never *ever* allow the weasel to perform "Steam Heat" in Vegas.

If that ever happens, Ramtha said, he would *not* be responsible for the consequences.

I'm joking, of course, about Shirley. She can do "Steam Heat" all she wants, because she was the first stranger I ever allowed to touch all my chakras, and afterwards I attained the highest state of spiritual consciousness of my entire life.

It started when I got this little book for Christmas called *Crystal Love* that had a red rock included with it and it's about how to use the earth's magic energy to fill my life with love and success, and I've gone through the entire program now and I've got to admit, it really works. Here's what happened to me. It can happen to you, too.

First I put my red crystal rock in the palm of my hand and let the water run over it and wash all the *old* energy into nothingness, and then I buried the rock in a bed of sea salt for seven days and during that time I let no impure thoughts come into my mind. I went through the entire *Family Affair* rerun plots, except for the ones where Buffy is mean to Mister French.

Now I was ready to make contact with my love stone. So I sat by the window and put the stone over my heart and took eighty-seven deep breaths and imagined that I was filled up inside with a pink light and that I was starting to hear my inner voice for the first time. It was tiny at first, but it got stronger and stronger. My inner voice was saying, "You got a rock on your chest."

Next I started talkin to the rock, telling it what I wanted, *visualizing* my dream as reality, tellin it stuff like "I already have my heart's desire, and she has a couple of forty-fours on her, that's how I'll know her when I see her coming." And then I tossed the rock around from hand to hand to send some love energy out to this humongously talented sleaze-a-rama sex machine with no known venereal diseases.

Now it gets complicated right in here, where you have to lay down a lot and stick the rock on top of your chakras, which are basically these zones on your body where if you get hit there with a baseball bat, you'll die. So you stick the rock on these places and it teaches you how to love yourself. I wanted a whole bunch of this part, so I did it eight, nine days, stickin that rock in places some people never even *thought* of stickin it, so that I could love *all* of myself. In fact, I got to where I liked this part of it so much that after a week or so, it was all I did all day long.

I'd lay down on a flat surface, start deep breathing with the rock on my Number One Chakra, which can be real ticklish, and work all the way up to Numero Seven, and on each one I'd be sendin out unconditional love to myself and forgivin the whole world and lovin my child-self and gettin rid of jealousy in people that aren't as nice as me and maybe don't have a love rock and releasin my anger and creatin all the prosperity I deserve and de-programmin all my negative self-judgments and generally makin myself into one heavy dude with a rock.

I guess it was last Thursday when it all hit me and I got the hunnerd percent pure-dee vision of the reality and fullness of what I was doing, and I was *one* with the rock and I knew there was no turning back cause it was *revealed* to me just exactly what the rock was meant to be in my life. And so I pressed the rock deeply into my palm and I wrapped the hand closely around its smooth surface and then I got into my car and I drove all night up to New York City, meditating all the way on the rock that was surgin energy through me, and when I got to New York City I found somebody that told me where the woman lived that wrote the book *Crystal Love* and when she came out of her house the next morning I sailed the rock forty feet in a perfect arc that barely missed her seventh chakra cause she was bending over to pick up the paper, but it hit her right in the Hiney Chakra and caused a sound to come out of her Throat Chakra like a weasel with diarrhea in a blender. This is what that rock had been made for all along. This is what the rock god had intended.

It was the most transcendent religious experience of my entire life.

I treasure it.

I wallow in it.

And I offer it to you, now, as a parable of the wonders to come if you will find your Iron Joe Bob and trust him, always trust him, no matter what lies he tells you.

But wait—there's one more chapter in the Iron Joe Bob legend.

Withdrawing from the Woolly Forest

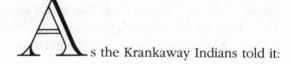s the Krankaway Indians told it:

The young brave thrust at the writhing monster for hours, then collapsed in the center of the forest, exhausted. He slept for a while, then woke up with the sun streaming onto his face. Suddenly everything in the forest looked different. He jumped up and ran out quickly. At the edge of the forest he was met by Iron Joe Bob, who stopped him and said, "Why do you run?" And the young brave said, "Because the forest looks a lot different after you get in there." And then Iron Joe Bob asked, "But where is your spear?" And the young brave said, "I know not." And Iron Joe Bob said, "You are now a man. You will find new spears, and they will all lead you into new forests, where you will wrestle with new and strange woolly monsters, and then you will run out again, agape." And the young man said, "Agape?" And Iron Joe Bob said, "Agape and agog, you will explore forests, but you will never under-

stand them and you will never conquer them. It is the fate of your kind." And the young man understood everything, and he said, "It sucks, doesn't it?" And Iron Joe Bob said, "Yes, it does." And the young man said, "I think I'll go back into the forest now." And Iron Joe Bob understood everything.

Why this epilogue to the Iron Joe Bob saga?

What does it mean?

Is something missing from the manuscript?

Will we ever know the whole story?

All I can do, to give you just a little bit of perspective, is to go back one more time to Chubb Fricke, the world's fattest ex-professional bowler. Because, even though Chubb is old and crotchety, even he was unable to resist modern spiritual trends.

About two months ago Chubb started giving one-hour seminars over at the Bronco Bowl where he could charge people 250 bucks to tell em how to wear rocks around their necks and make noises through their nose like a Hoover vacuum cleaner. It's something he read about in *Time* magazine. He calls it the Old Age Movement.

"Let us not walk in accordance with our grandkids who never call," Chubb starts out while everybody is settlin into their Lazy Boy recliners like beached whales. "Let us walk in the light of the TV with the cleansing power of Bob Barker, who is Spirit and God."

"And we?" the Old Age followers ask.

"Whatta ya want?" answers Chubb, in the traditional form of the Old Age ceremony.

"And we are Spirit and God as well?"

"We are full of white-bread products and liver disease and inflamed colons, and there dwells the spirit of Old Age."

"Heal us, Chubb!"

"No. Rather we shall ascend Mount Shasta and examine our colons together. Repeat after me: I feel *awful* today."

"I feel *awful* today."

"I think it was the mashed potatoes."

"It was the mashed potatoes."

"I got to stop eatin those lousy mashed potatoes."

"I got to stop eatin . . . "

"No! You are now kings in your own households!"

"Yes, Master Chubb."

"You are kings and you will reign as kings. You will watch the channel on the TV you want to watch. You will listen to the music you want to listen to. You will never leave the house when you *don't want to leave the house.* And it is given to you to know why all these things have come to pass."

"Yes, Master Chubb."

"Because you are *old.*"

"We are *old.*"

"You are so old you don't take guff off anybody. When the stock market plunges, you grin and say, 'Come take a look at this, honey, bunch of idiots in New York.' When Ramtha speaks, you respond, 'I got your Atlantis warrior right *here.*' And you are the chosen now. You are chosen to lead the multitudes toward the ultimate UFO experience. Are you ready?"

"We are ready, Master Chubb."

"It is time then. It is time to build a giant spaceship. It is time to build it strong and silver and shiny. It is time to put Shirley MacLaine in it and point her at Uranus."

"Now, Master Chubb?"

"First your 250 bucks. Okay. Now. Put the bimbo in orbit."

There is much we can learn from our elders.

To discuss the meaning of life with Joe Bob, or to get a copy of Joe Bob's world-famous newsletter, *We Are the Weird,* write Joe Bob Briggs, P.O. Box 2002, Dallas, TX 75221.